Cross Stitch is a timeless craft that brings a classic style to modern home décor. But, what if you branched out of your traditional cross stitch, and tried something colorful and fascinating? The subtle beauty of cross stitch on hand-dyed fabric transcends the concept of the craft and helps these beautiful patterns of flowers and leaves sparkle with their own unique colors. Add depth and originality to your cross stitch projects before you even thread the needle! Mix and match dyes with stitch patterns to see for yourself how fun and exciting these mixed media cross stitch projects can really be.

You'll quickly learn how to prepare your fabric and protect your clothing and work surfaces. Then it's as easy as placing the dye on the fabric! To showcase the flowers or leaves, use Rit® Dye to "paint" a distinctive background on ordinary 14 count Aida fabric. Your creations are guaranteed to be original, and our easy-to-follow instructions ensure your success! Discover the satisfying results of this "color enhanced" cross stitch.

Leisure Arts, Inc.
Maumelle, Arkansas

DYEING INSTRUCTIONS

GATHER YOUR SUPPLIES

YOU WILL NEED:

- ◊ Newspaper
- ◊ Plastic wrap
- ◊ A cookie sheet or jelly roll pan
- ◊ Measuring cup
- ◊ Measuring spoons
- ◊ Lots of white paper towels
- ◊ Containers for mixing dyes
- ◊ Spoons to stir dyes
- ◊ Rubber gloves
- ◊ Apron
- ◊ Salt
- ◊ Rit® Dye (see each project for specific colors)
- ◊ White Aida fabric for practicing dyeing
- ◊ White Aida fabric for stitching

PREPARING YOUR FABRIC

To mark area to be dyed, work basting stitches along stitch count lines. Mark top of fabric with a thread "X."

Wash fabric in cool water with a mild dish washing detergent to remove sizing. Rinse well. Press fabric to remove wrinkles, but do not press fabric dry. You want your fabric to be damp.

PREPARING WORK AREA

Since dyes are made to color anything they come in contact with, you'll need to protect your work area. Layer plastic wrap, then paper towels on your countertops. Place newspaper, then plastic wrap, and finally paper towels on your cookie sheet. Place dampened, basted Aida on paper towels. Put on your rubber gloves and apron.

MIXING DYES

We used Rit Dyes, mostly powder dyes, but a few liquid ones as well. Refer to the project instructions for specific colors and measurements when mixing dyes. When using powder dyes, be sure to use very hot water (approx. 140°F) and to mix until the dye powder and the salt are dissolved.

DYEING FABRIC

Begin with the lightest color of dye. Dip a damp, crumpled paper towel in dye. Lightly dab dye onto the damp Aida. Color will spread as dye is absorbed into the fabric.

Practice dabbing dye onto fabric, using a new damp paper towel for each color of dye. Try dabbing harder to see if color spreads differently. You may also slightly overlap dye as you dab. Also try lightly rubbing the dye onto the fabric; this technique will give you a softer, more blended look.

You don't have to wait for colors to dry before adding the next dye color. Colors will dry more vividly than they look when wet. Allow fabric to dry overnight.

SETTING THE DYE

Remove excess dye from fabric by holding fabric under cold running water and allowing water to flow through fabric. Rinse for approximately 2 minutes. Do not wring fabric. Place between several layers of paper towels to blot excess water.

Protect your ironing board cover with several layers of paper towels. Use additional paper towels to protect iron. With iron on cotton setting, press fabric dry. Don't use steam. Use lift and press motions, rather than back and forth motions.

When disposing of dye, slowly pour it directly down the drain and rinse your sink well.

Now you have created a one-of-a-kind piece of fabric for your stitching. Since you will not be able to wash your completed stitched piece, try to keep the fabric as flat as possible while stitching.

tip

You will want to practice on leftover or scrap Aida to get a feel for how the dye moves on the fabric and how much dye to use.

When applying dye, refer to photo of the finished piece and instructional photos.

It is easier to have all of your supplies ready and at hand when dyeing.

WINTER HOLLY

RIT® DYE POWDER COLORS NEEDED

- ◊ Lemon Yellow
- ◊ Golden Yellow
- ◊ Tangerine
- ◊ Cherry Red Liquid Dye
- ◊ Fuchsia
- ◊ Cocoa Brown

PREPPING YOUR FABRIC

Cut a piece of 14 count White Aida 12½"w x 11"h. Stitch count is 89w x 69h; work basting stitches to define dye area. Wash, rinse and press.

MIXING THE DYE

COLOR	DYE	WATER	SALT
lemon yellow	1 teaspoon	1 cup	1 teaspoon
golden yellow	1 teaspoon	1 cup	1 teaspoon
tangerine	1 teaspoon	1 cup	1 teaspoon
cherry red & fuchsia	3 teaspoons & ½ teaspoon	1 cup	1 teaspoon
cocoa brown	1 teaspoon	1 cup	1 teaspoon

We dyed and stitched Winter Holly as charted (horizontally) and framed it vertically.

ONE Beginning with lemon yellow, dab dye on the top center of the fabric, moving toward the right side.

TWO Dab golden yellow on the lower portion of fabric, going back up on the right to meet the lemon yellow. Add some color to the upper left side.

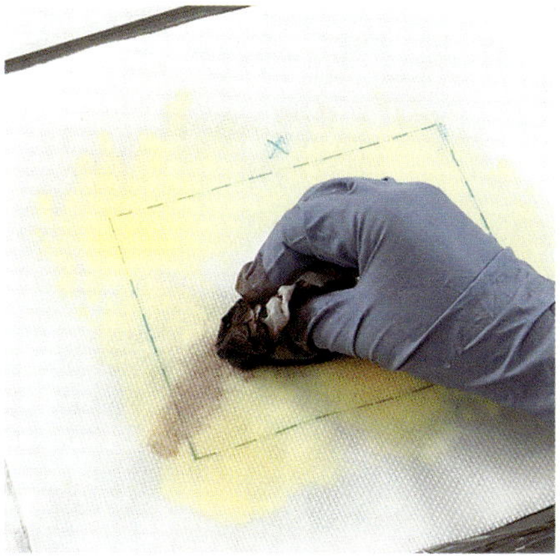

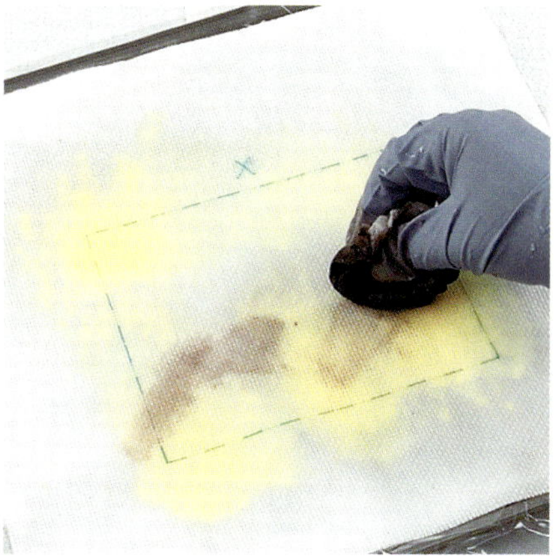

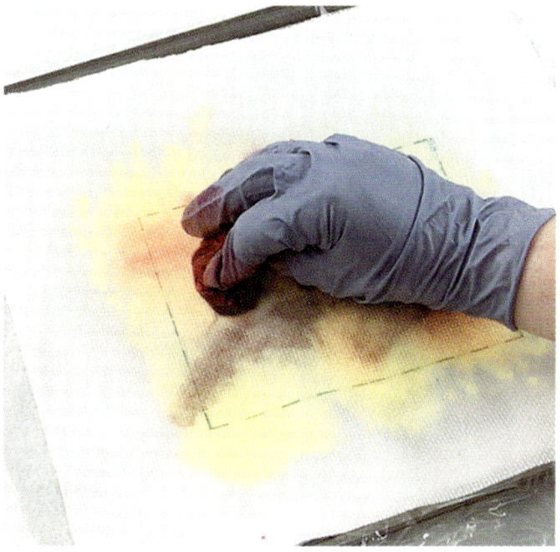

THREE Add some cocoa brown to the lower left and fade it out toward the center.

FOUR Dab tangerine and cherry red/fuchsia mixture in the upper left corner and near the middle. Add a bit of color to the lower right corner. Make sure color extends at least 1" beyond basting threads.

FIVE Allow to dry overnight. You may add more dye if you wish, but be sure to dampen your fabric first and mix up new dye. When you are happy with the look of your fabric, set the dye. You are now ready to begin stitching.

Winter Holly

x	dmc	b'st	color
C	165		lt yellow green
T	349		dk coral
☆	350		coral
↑	351		lt coral
H	420	/	hazel
+	700		green
4	702		dk yellow green
7	704		yellow green
a	816	/	red
Z	910		lt green
X	912		dk emerald
8	954		emerald
V	955		lt emerald
2	3051		avocado
√	3818	/	dk green
◊	3828	/	lt hazel
n	3865		white
•	3865		white Fr. Knot

Grey area indicates last row of previous section of design.

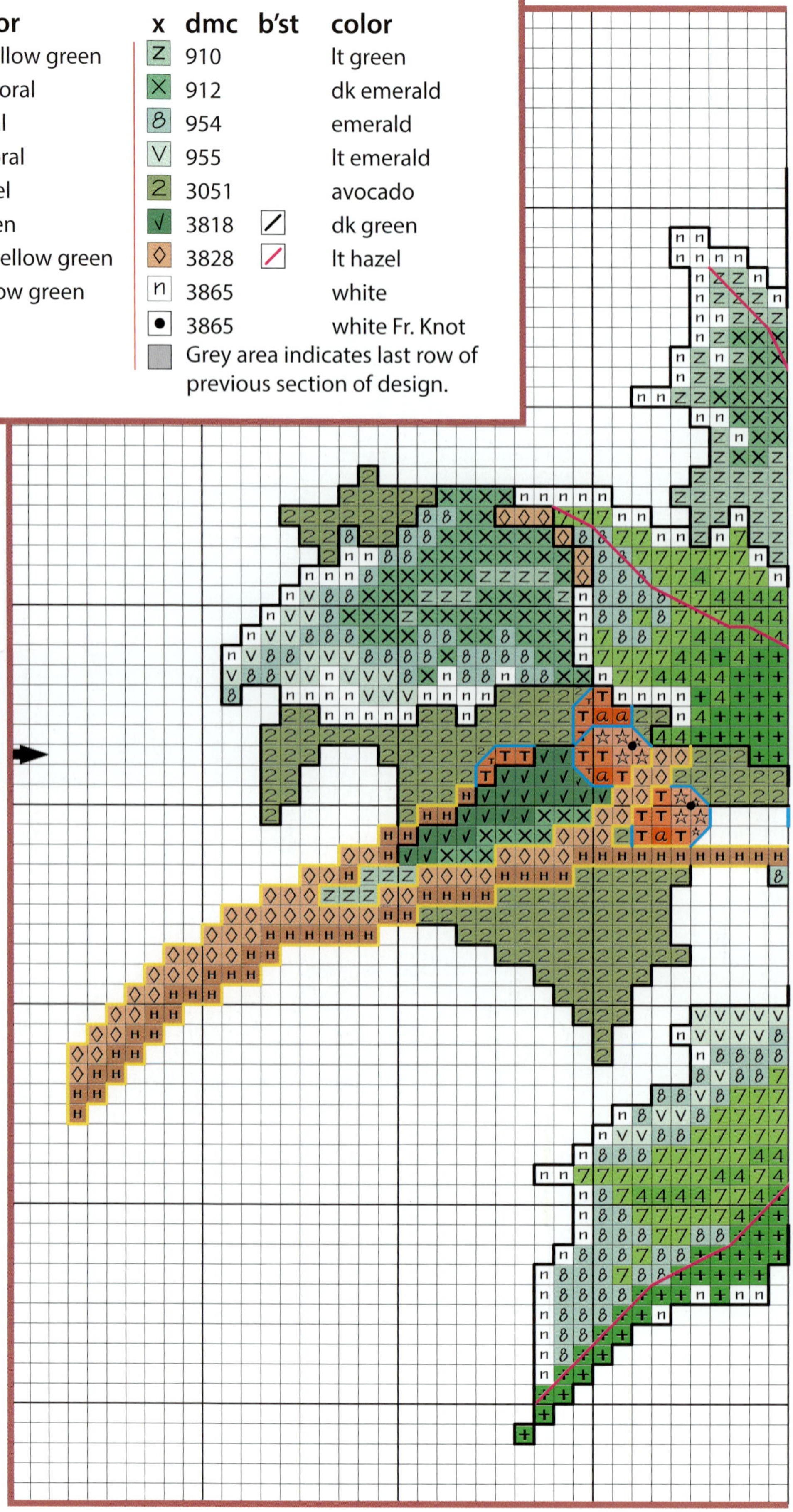

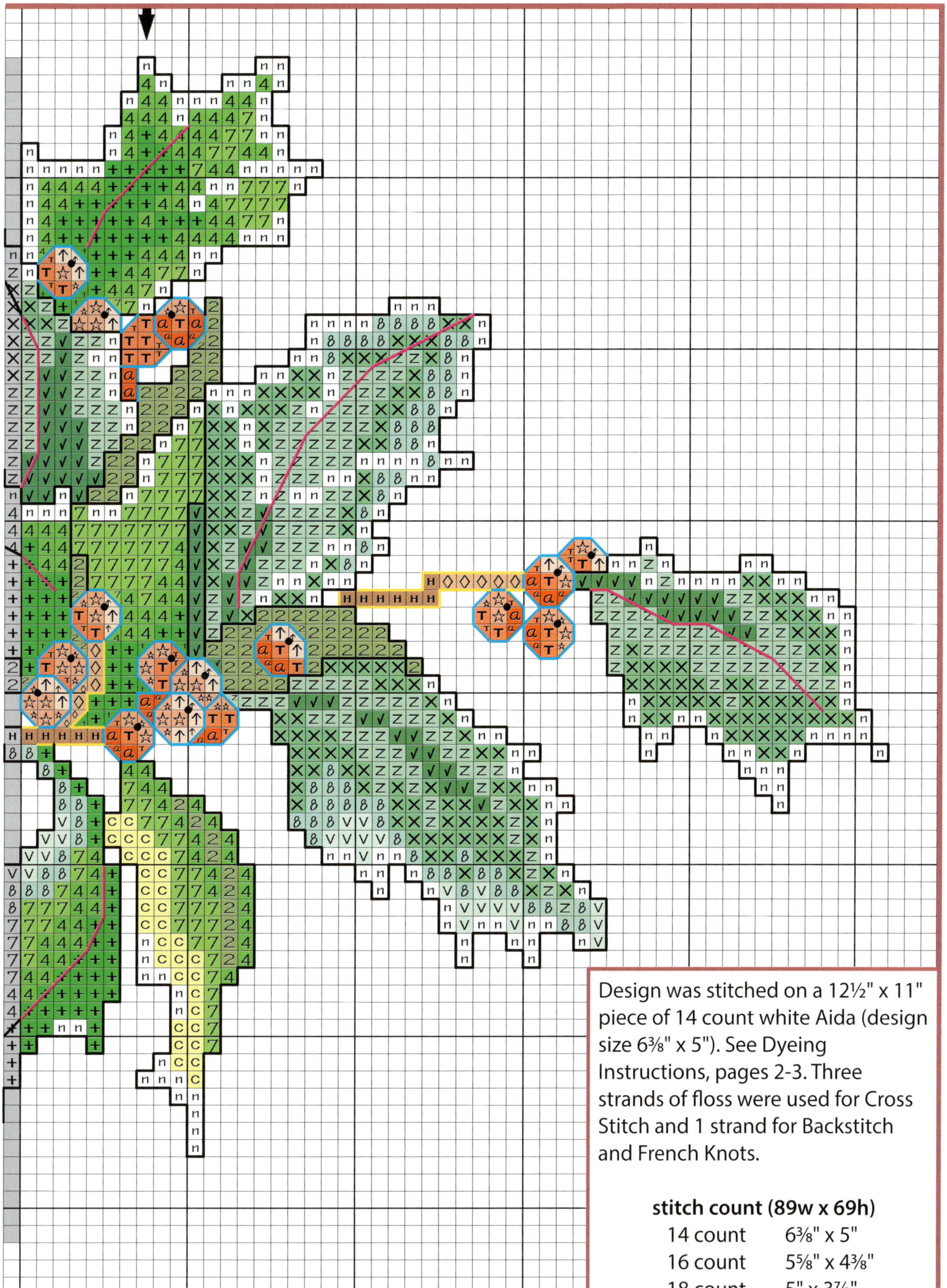

Design was stitched on a 12½" x 11" piece of 14 count white Aida (design size 6⅜" x 5"). See Dyeing Instructions, pages 2-3. Three strands of floss were used for Cross Stitch and 1 strand for Backstitch and French Knots.

stitch count (89w x 69h)

14 count	6⅜" x 5"
16 count	5⅝" x 4⅜"
18 count	5" x 3⅞"

SPRING DAFFODIL

RIT® DYE POWDER COLORS NEEDED

- ◊ Lemon Yellow
- ◊ Kelly Green
- ◊ Dark Green
- ◊ Evening Blue Liquid Dye
- ◊ Denim Blue
- ◊ Royal Blue

PREPPING YOUR FABRIC

Cut a piece of 14 count White Aida 10½"w x 11½"h. Stitch count is 61w x 76h; work basting stitches to define dye area. Wash, rinse and press.

MIXING THE DYE

COLOR	DYE	WATER	SALT
lemon yellow & kelly green	½ teaspoon & ⅛ teaspoon	1 cup	1 teaspoon
dark green	1 teaspoon	1 cup	1 teaspoon
evening blue	4 teaspoons	1 cup	1 teaspoon
denim blue	1 teaspoon	1 cup	1 teaspoon
royal blue	1 teaspoon	1 cup	1 teaspoon

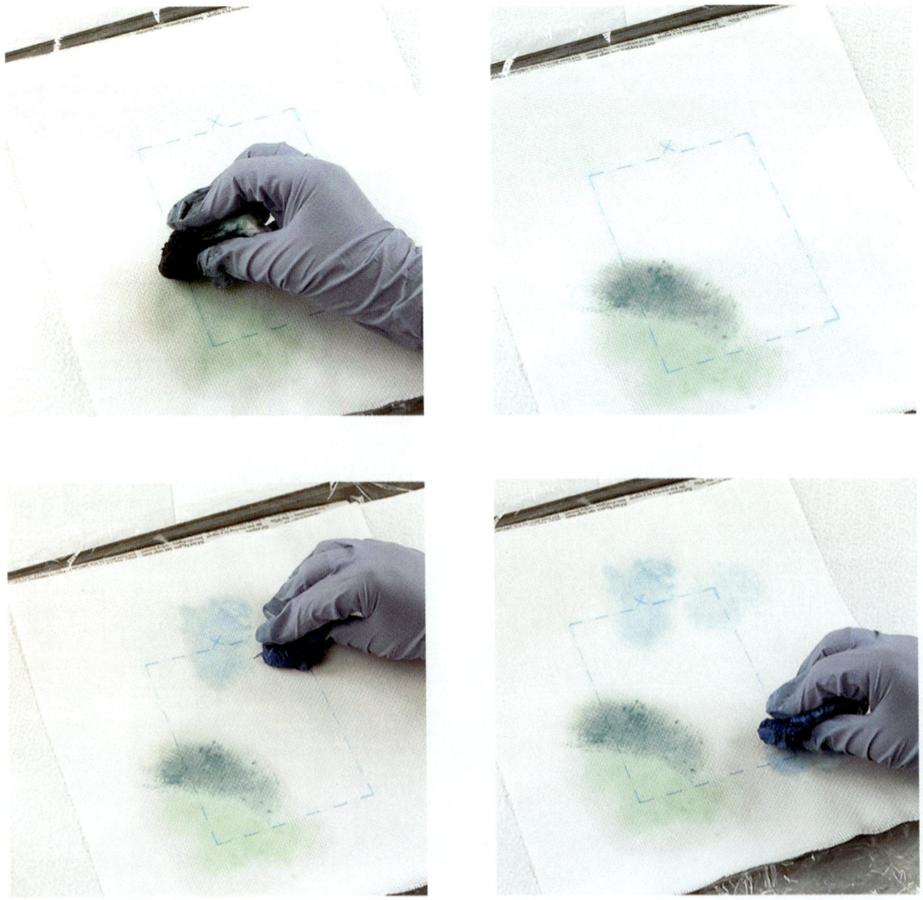

ONE Beginning with lemon yellow/kelly green mixture, dab dye on the lower left side of the fabric. Dab dark green dye down toward center on left side.

TWO Dab evening blue on the top center and top right of fabric. Add some color along the bottom right corner.

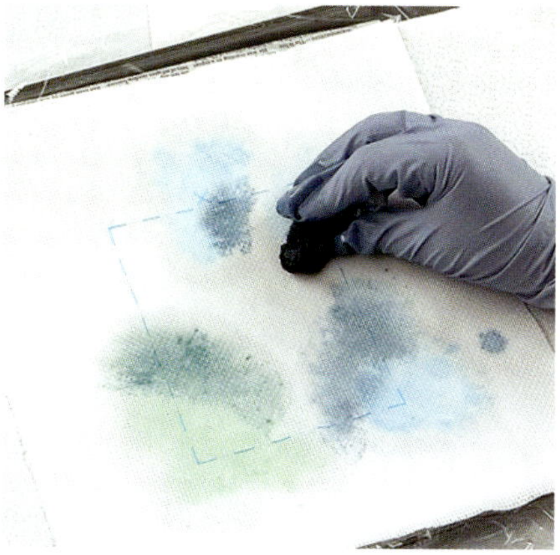

THREE Dab denim blue along the right edge, going toward the top edge. Dab royal blue here and there along the same areas, allowing some of the denim blue to show through. Add royal blue along the left edge. Make sure color extends at least 1" beyond basting threads.

FOUR Allow to dry overnight. You may add more dye if you wish, but be sure to dampen your fabric first and mix up new dye. When you are happy with the look of your fabric, set the dye. You are now ready to begin stitching.

Spring Daffodil

x	dmc	b'st	color
a	164		mint green
L	165		lt yellow green
H	166		yellow green
√	319	/	dk green
X	320		lt green
Z	367		green
✳	370		hazel
S	469		avocado
V	581		dk yellow green
	606	/	dk orange
♡	608	/	orange
∩	642	/	beige
+	644		lt beige
T	729		gold
8	740		lt orange
4	742		dk yellow
7	743		yellow
1	744		lt yellow
n	746		cream
●	772		lt mint green
=	834		lt hazel
	936	/	dk avocado
2	3011	/	khaki
m	3347		dk mint green
★	3810		blue
◇	3821		lt gold
☆	3865		lt white
●	746		cream Fr. Knot

Grey area indicates last row of previous section of design.

Design was stitched on a 10½" x 11½" piece of 14 count white Aida (design size 4⅜" x 5½"). See Dyeing Instructions, pages 2-3. Three strands of floss were used for Cross Stitch and 1 strand for Backstitch and French Knots.

stitch count (61wx 76h)

14 count	4⅜" x 5½"
16 count	3⅞" x 4¾"
18 count	3½" x 4¼"

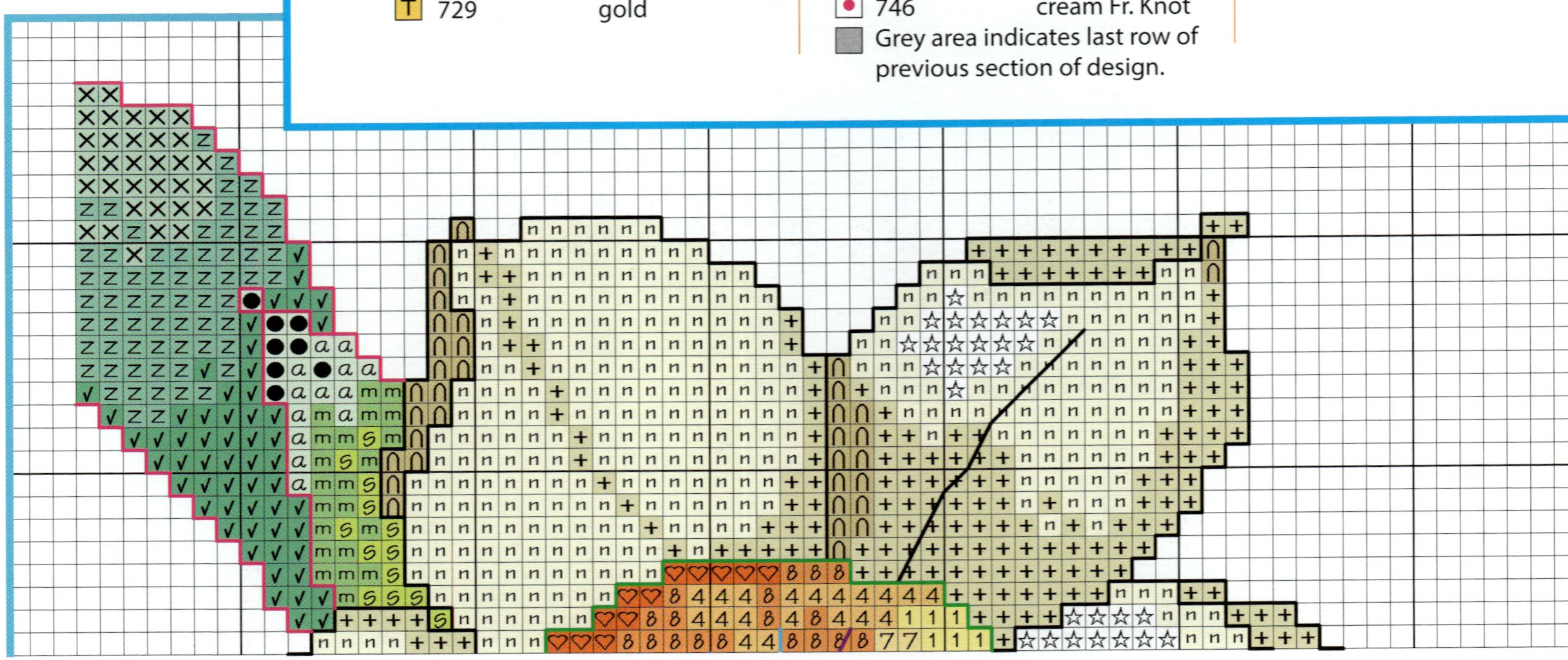

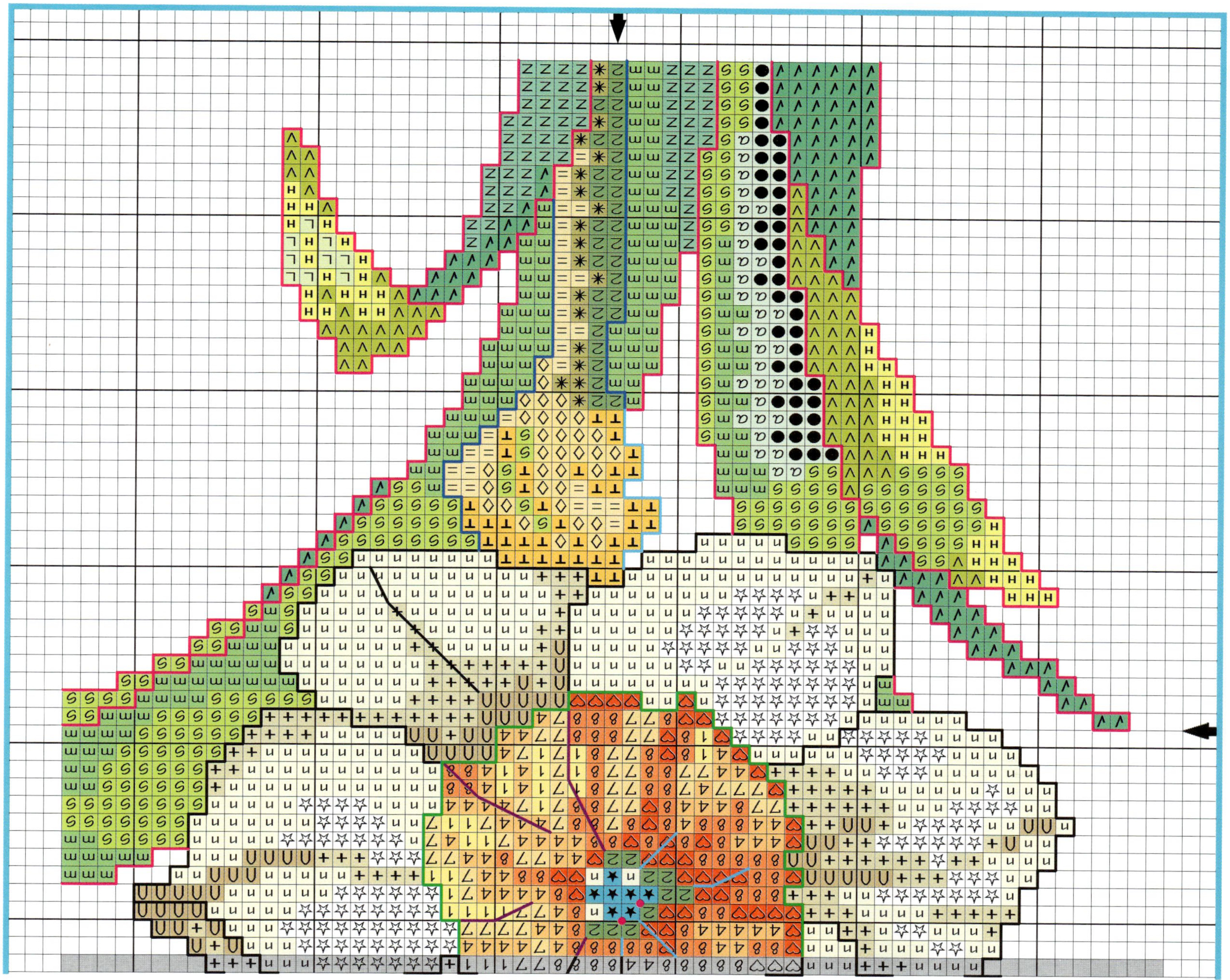

SUMMER ROSE

RIT® DYE POWDER COLORS NEEDED

- ◊ Lemon Yellow
- ◊ Kelly Green
- ◊ Dark Green
- ◊ Evening Blue Liquid Dye

PREPPING YOUR FABRIC

Cut a piece of 14 count White Aida 12½"w x 10½"h. Stitch count is 87w x 59h; work basting stitches to define dye area. Wash, rinse and press.

MIXING THE DYE

COLOR	DYE	WATER	SALT
lemon yellow & kelly green	1 teaspoon & ¼ teaspoon	1 cup	1 teaspoon
kelly green	1 teaspoon	1 cup	1 teaspoon
dark green	1 teaspoon	1 cup	1 teaspoon
evening blue	4 teaspoons	1 cup	1 teaspoon

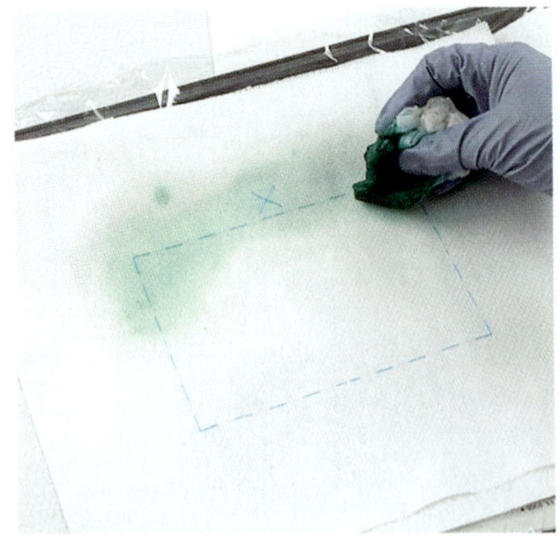

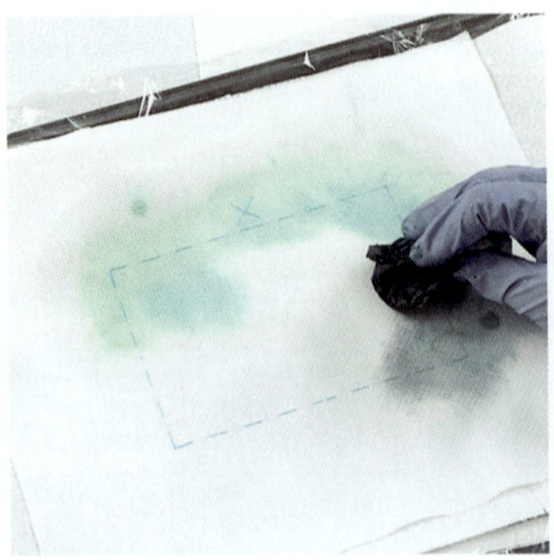

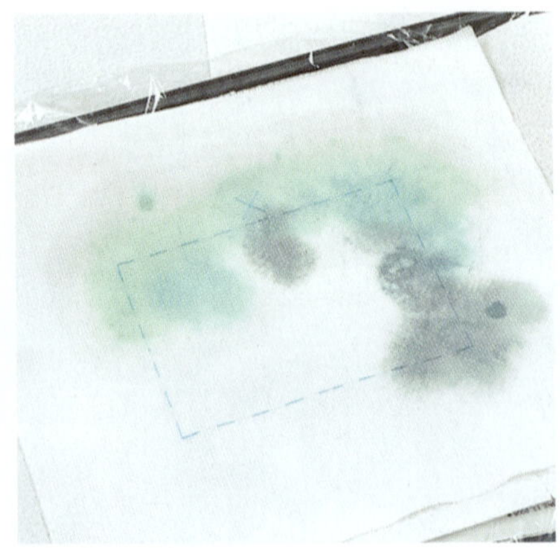

ONE Beginning with lemon yellow/kelly green mixture, dab dye on the upper edges of the fabric.

TWO Dab kelly green along the upper edges of the fabric, allowing lemon yellow/kelly green mixture to show through. Add some dark green here and there among the other greens and at the bottom right corner.

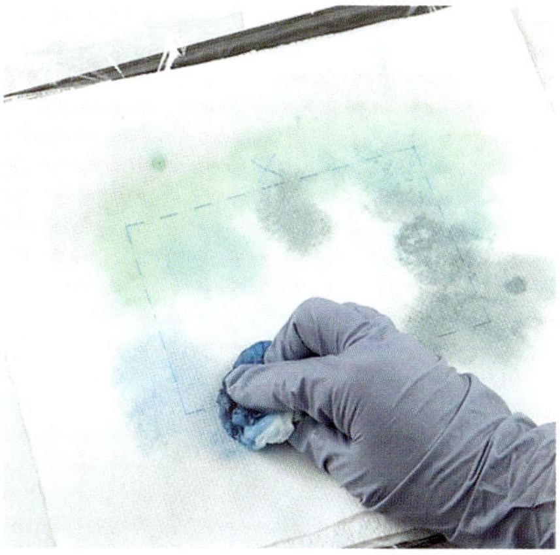

THREE Dab evening blue on the lower left corner of the fabric and along the bottom edge. Make sure color extends at least 1" beyond basting threads.

FOUR Allow to dry overnight. You may add more dye if you wish, but be sure to dampen your fabric first and mix up new dye. When you are happy with the look of your fabric, set the dye. You are now ready to begin stitching.

Summer Rose

x	dmc	b'st	color
–	165		dk yellow green
Z	347		red
X	351		dk coral
O	352		coral
V	353		lt coral
	355	/	terra cotta
*	367		green
√	500	/	blue green
2	501		lt blue green
H	744		yellow
L	745		lt yellow
n	746		cream
◊	906		dk yellow green
#	986		dk green
+	3347		lt green
/	3819		yellow green
S	3856		peach

Grey area indicates last row of previous section of design.

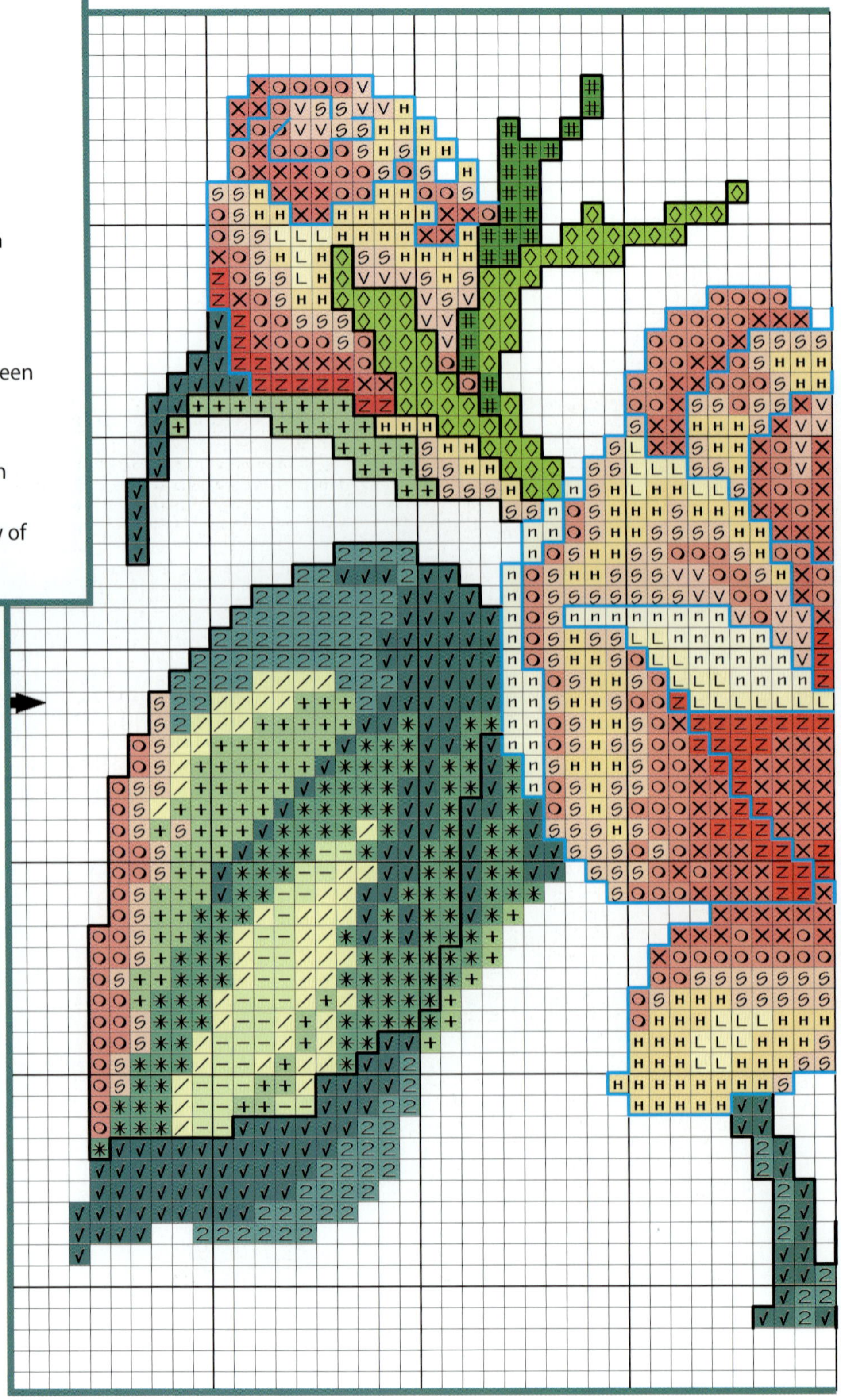

Design was stitched on a 12½" x 10½" piece of 14 count white Aida (design size 6¼" x 4¼"). See Dyeing Instructions, pages 2-3. Three strands of floss were used for Cross Stitch and 1 strand for Backstitch.

stitch count (87w x 59h)

14 count	6¼" x 4¼"
16 count	5½" x 3¾"
18 count	4⅞" x 3⅜"

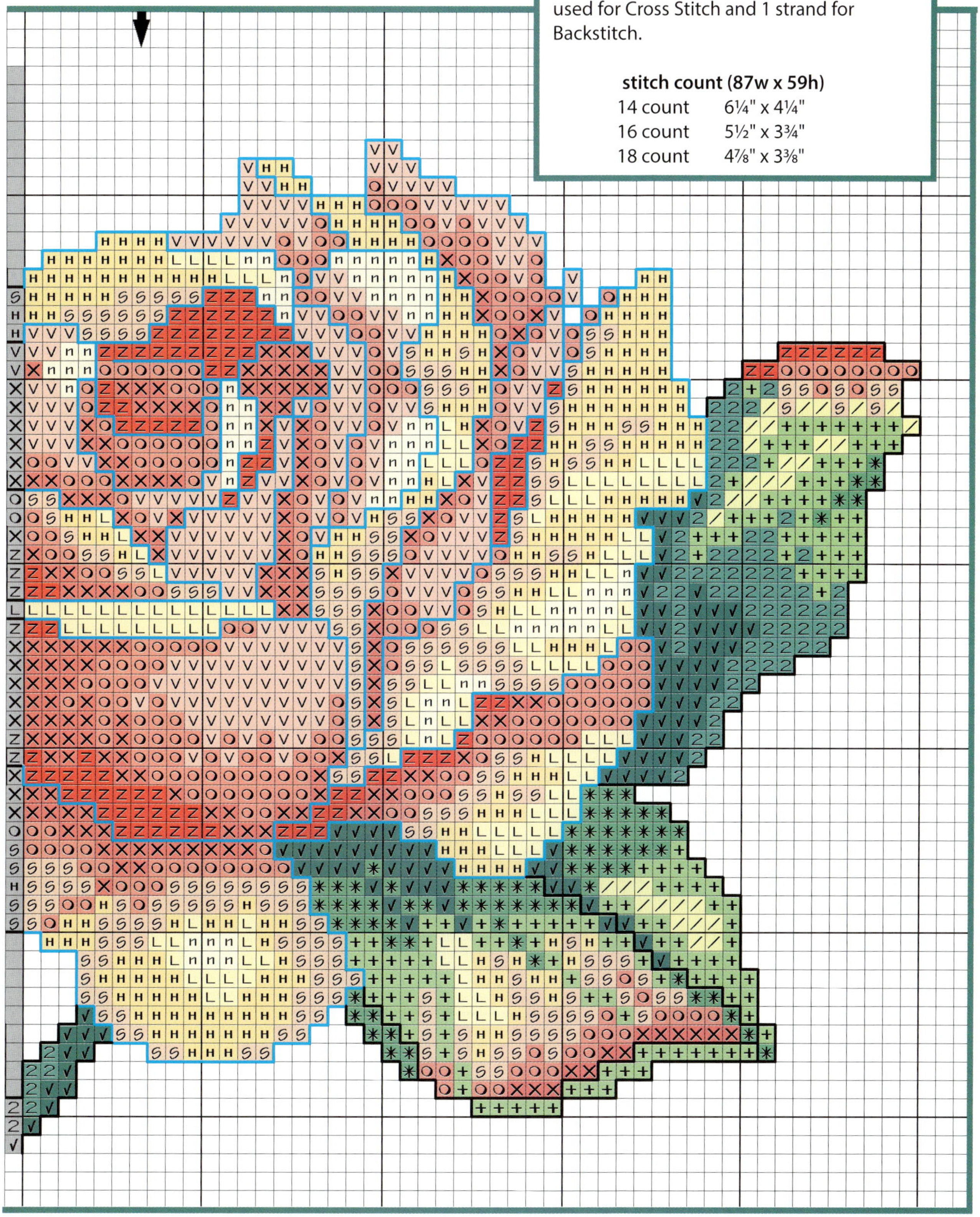

AUTUMN LEAVES

RIT® DYE POWDER COLORS NEEDED

- ◊ Lemon Yellow
- ◊ Golden Yellow
- ◊ Denim Blue
- ◊ Kelly Green
- ◊ Dark Green

PREPPING YOUR FABRIC

Cut a piece of 14 count White Aida 12½"w x 11½"h. Stitch count is 89w x 71h; work basting stitches to define dye area. Wash, rinse and press.

MIXING THE DYE

COLOR	DYE	WATER	SALT
lemon yellow & kelly green	1 teaspoon & ¼ teaspoon	1 cup	1 teaspoon
golden yellow	1 teaspoon	1 cup	1 teaspoon
denim blue	1 teaspoon	1 cup	1 teaspoon
golden yellow & dark green	1 teaspoon & ½ teaspoon	1 cup	1 teaspoon

We dyed and stitched Autumn Leaves as charted (horizontally) and framed it vertically.

ONE Beginning with lemon yellow/kelly green mixture, dab dye on the upper right corner of the fabric. Add more color in the lower corners and along the right edge.

TWO Dab golden yellow near the bottom center of the fabric. Add some color to the upper left toward the center of the fabric.

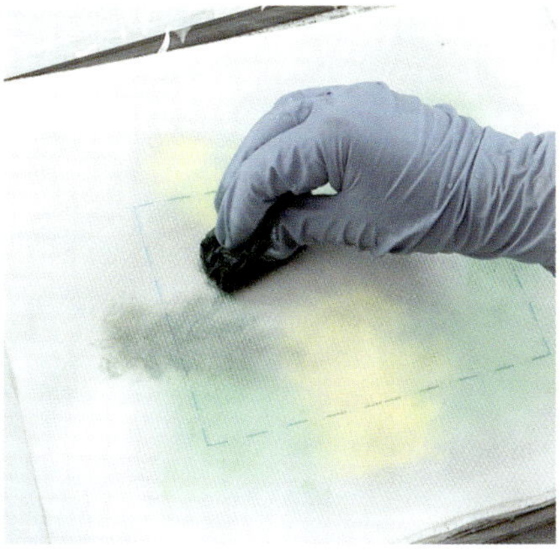

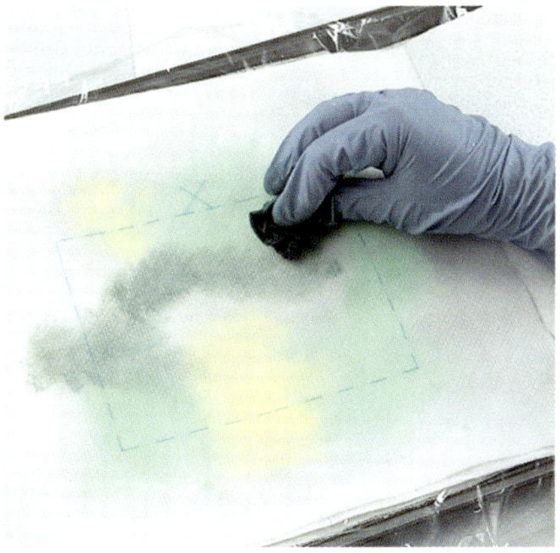

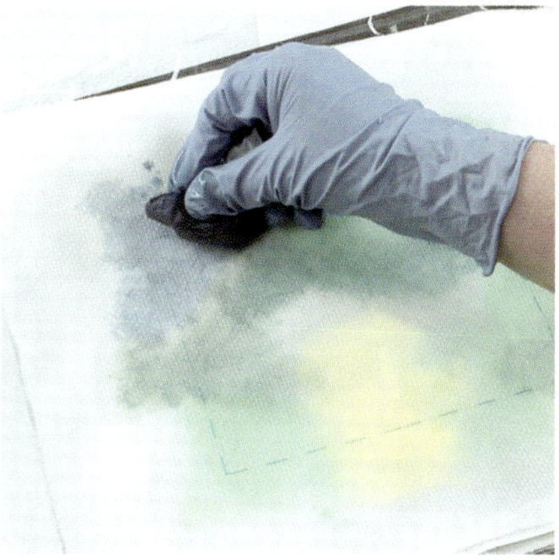

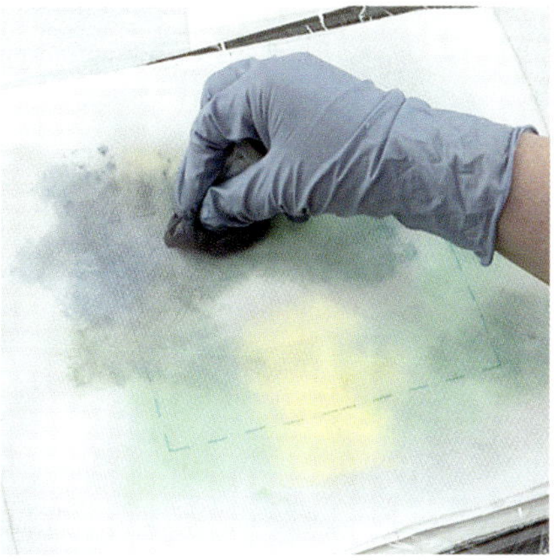

THREE Dab golden yellow/dark green mixture between the golden yellow and the lighter green mixture. Add darker green mixture through the middle area.

FOUR Dab denim blue in the upper left corner, extending slightly toward the bottom and the center. Make sure color extends at least 1" beyond basting threads.

FIVE Allow to dry overnight. You may add more dye if you wish, but be sure to dampen your fabric first and mix up new dye. When you are happy with the look of your fabric, set the dye. You are now ready to begin stitching.

Autumn Leaves

x	dmc	b'st	color
V	722		vy lt copper
8	729		gold
a	918	/	vy dk copper
Z	920		dk copper
X	921		copper
2	922		lt copper
∩	3781	/	brown
4	3821		dk yellow
7	3822		yellow
+	3823		lt yellow
↑	3824		peach
H	3854		orange
m	3855		lt orange
✳	3862		lt brown

Grey area indicates last row of previous section of design.

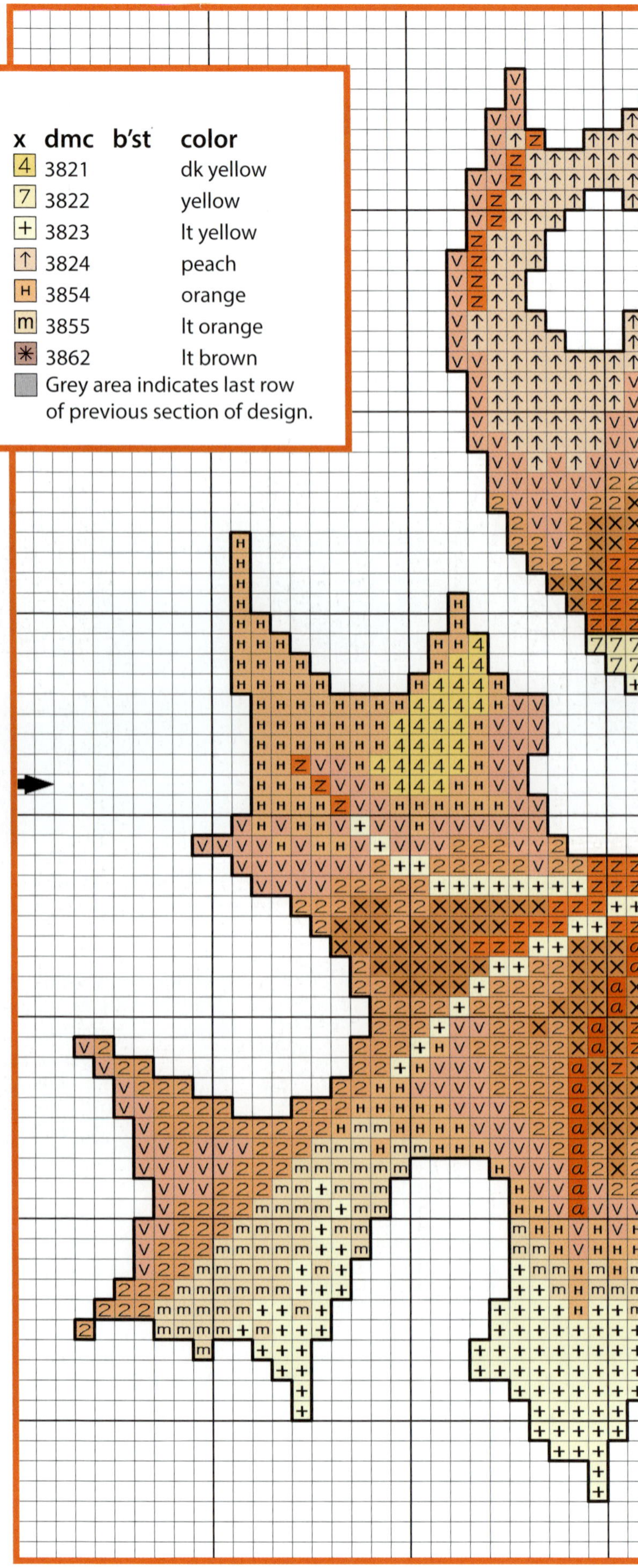

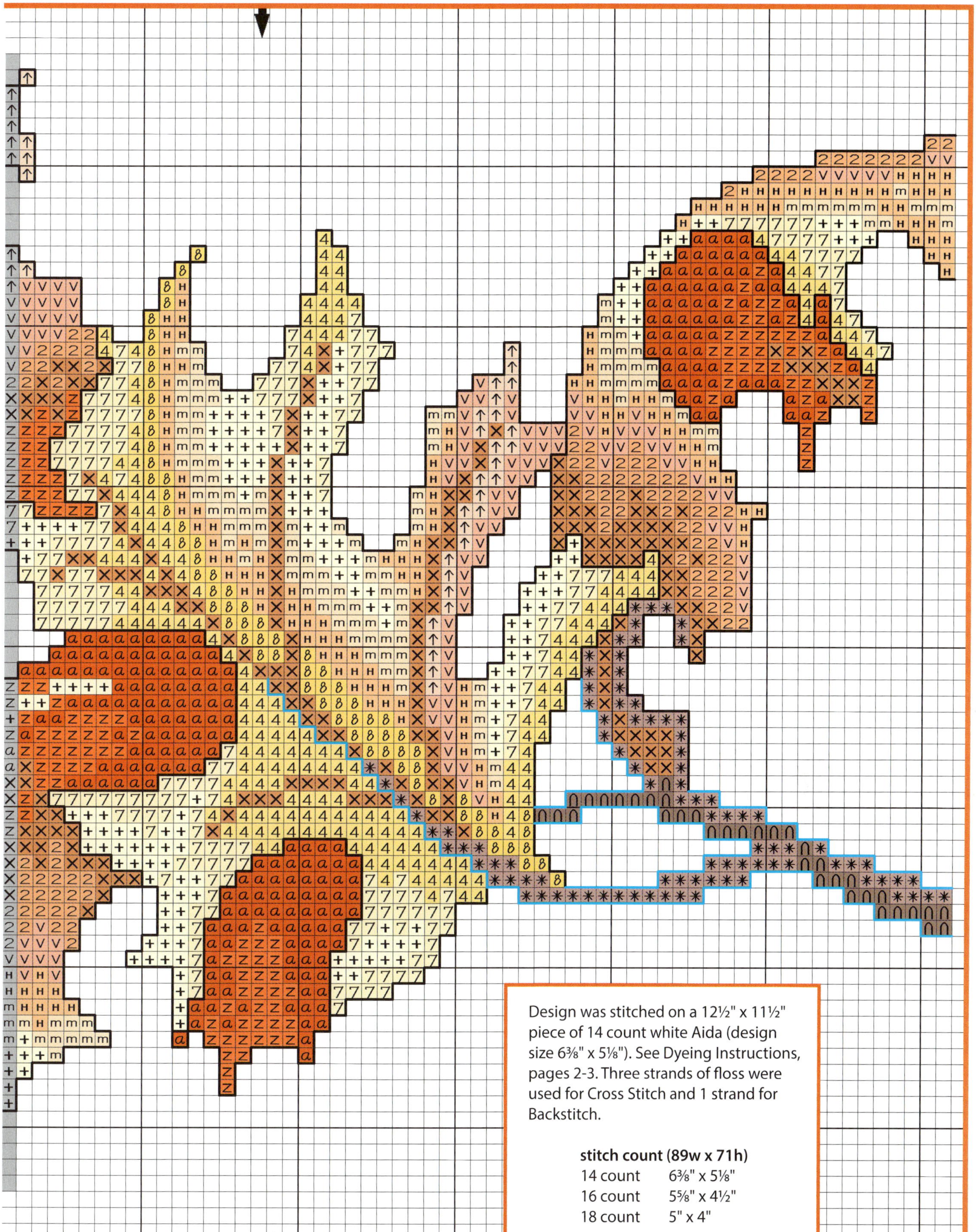

Design was stitched on a 12½" x 11½" piece of 14 count white Aida (design size 6⅜" x 5⅛"). See Dyeing Instructions, pages 2-3. Three strands of floss were used for Cross Stitch and 1 strand for Backstitch.

stitch count (89w x 71h)

14 count	6⅜" x 5⅛"
16 count	5⅝" x 4½"
18 count	5" x 4"

HIBISCUS

RIT® DYE POWDER COLORS NEEDED

- ◊ Evening Blue Liquid Dye
- ◊ Royal Blue
- ◊ Purple

PREPPING YOUR FABRIC

Cut a piece of 14 count White Aida $12^1/_2$"w x $11^1/_2$"h. Stitch count is 86w x 71h; work basting stitches to define dye area. Wash, rinse and press.

MIXING THE DYE

COLOR	DYE	WATER	SALT
evening blue	4 teaspoons	1 cup	1 teaspoon
royal blue	1 teaspoon	1 cup	1 teaspoon
purple	1 teaspoon	1 cup	1 teaspoon

ONE Beginning with evening blue, dab dye on the right side of the fabric and across the bottom edge then up the left side of the fabric and across to the center top side.

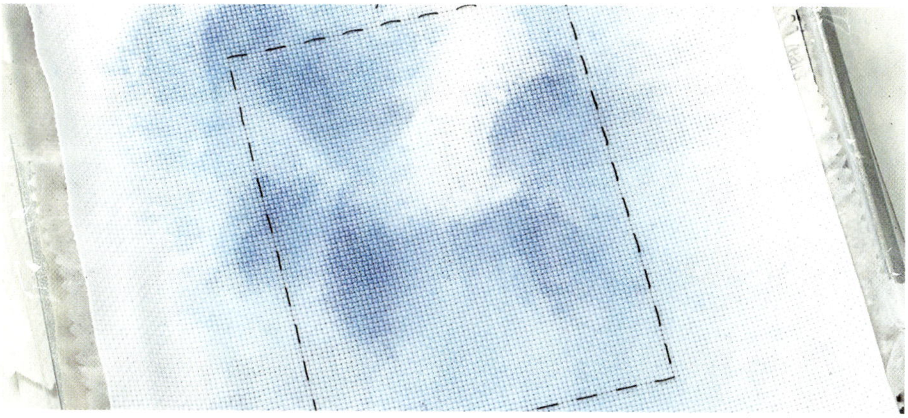

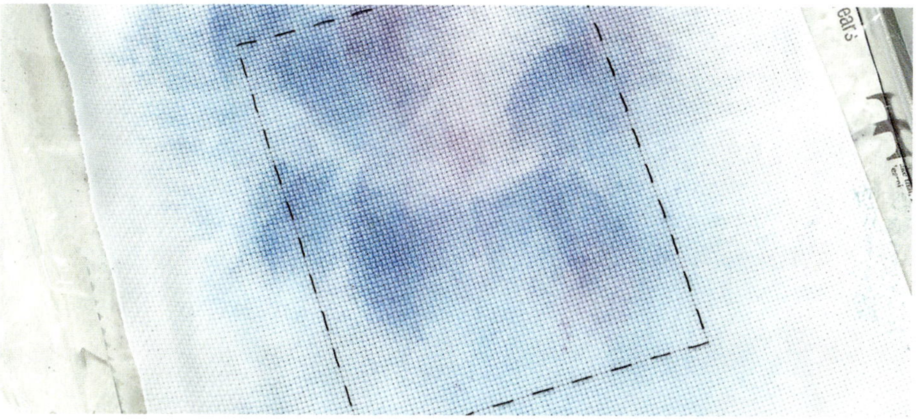

TWO Dab royal blue across center of fabric and up slightly on each side to blend with the evening blue. Dab royal blue from center of fabric curving upwards to top left corner.

THREE Dab purple to top center. Add some purple along right side to areas where blues meet. Gently rub to blend colors.

FOUR Allow to dry overnight. You may add more dye if you wish, but be sure to dampen the fabric first and mix up new dye. When you are happy with the look of your fabric, set the dye. You are now ready to begin stitching.

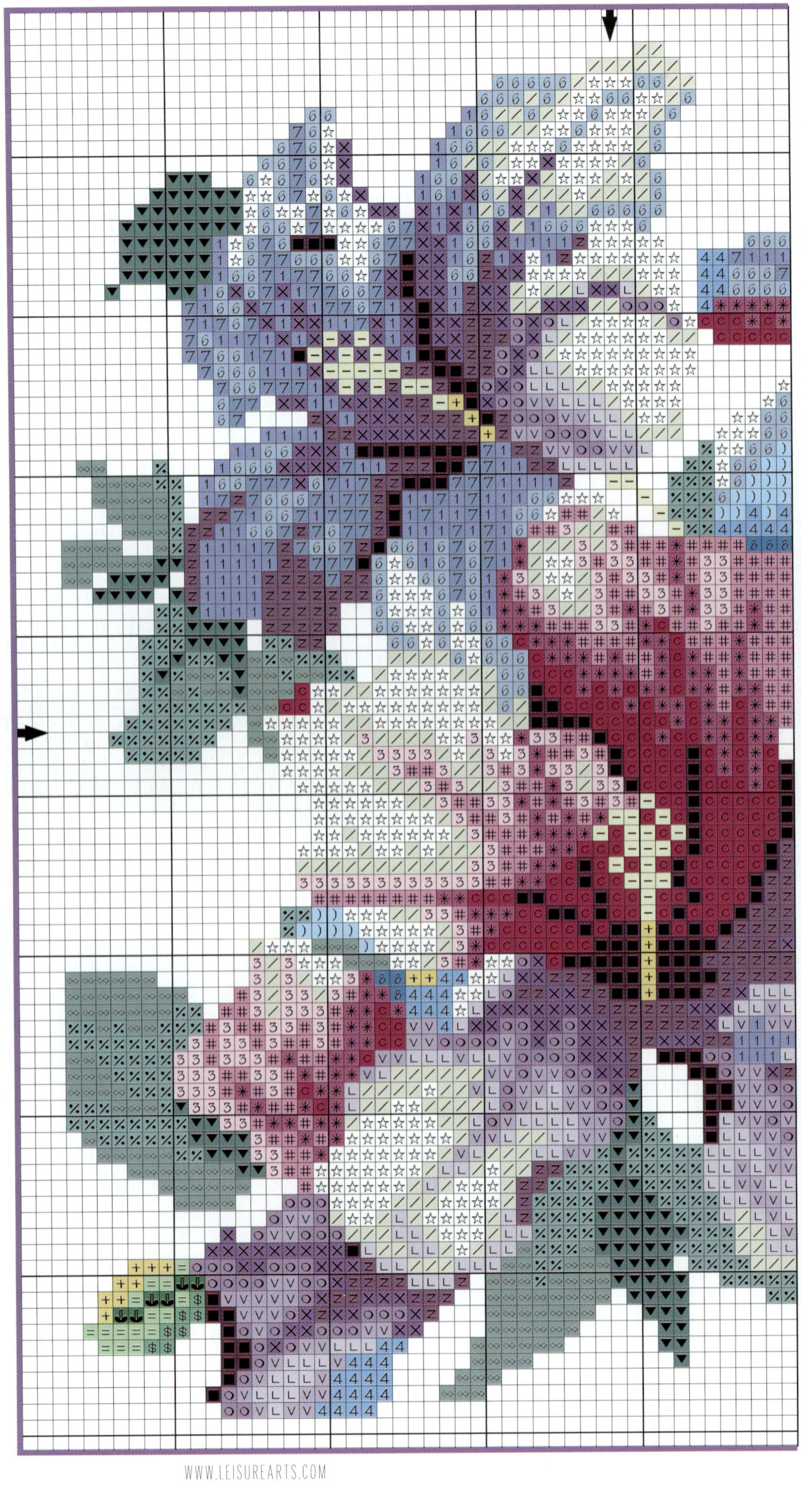

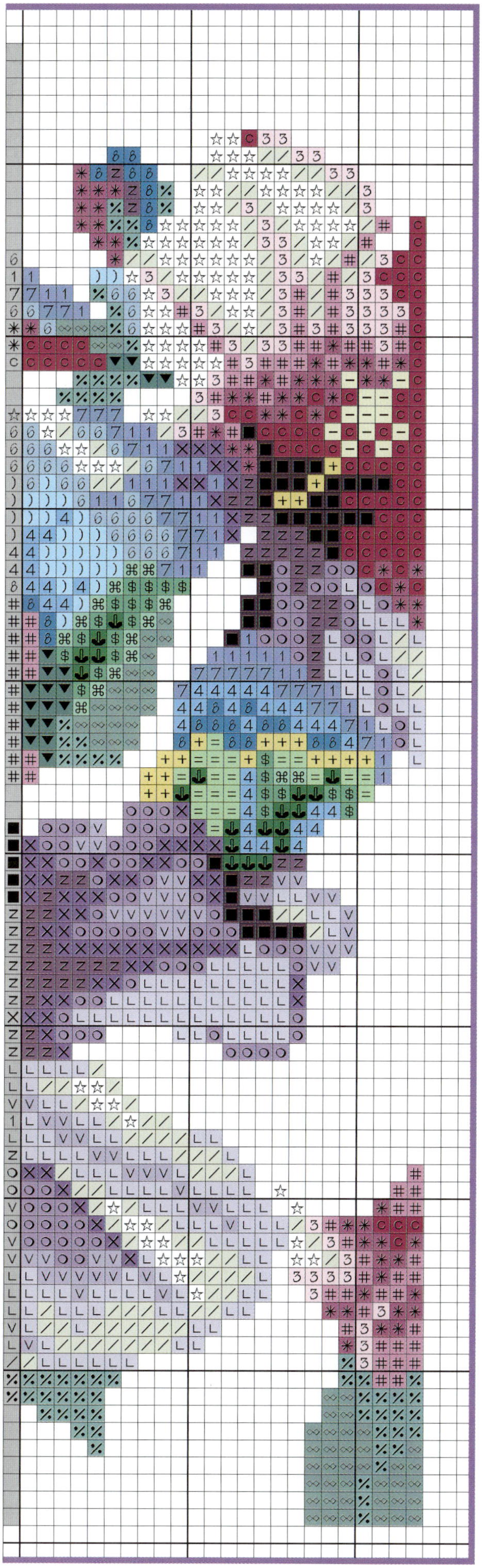

Hibiscus

x	dmc	color
■	154	dk purple
7	156	lt blue violet
6	157	baby blue
$	163	green
=	164	yellow green
X	208	dk lavender
O	209	lavender
V	210	lt lavender
L	211	vy lt lavender
8	312	dk blue
4	322	blue
Z	327	purple
1	340	blue violet
⚓	561	dk green
⌘	563	lt green
C	915	dk fuchsia
▼	924	dk grey green
∞	926	lt grey green
✱	3607	dk fuchsia
#	3608	fuchsia
3	3609	lt fuchsia
)	3755	lt blue
%	3768	grey green
+	3822	yellow
−	3823	lt yellow
☆	3865	white
/	3866	tan

Grey area indicates last row of previous section of design.

Design was stitched on a 12½" x 11½" piece of 14 count white Aida (design size 6¼" x 5¼"). See Dyeing Instructions, pages 2-3. Three strands of floss were used for Cross Stitch.

stitch count (86w x 71h)

14 count	6¼" x 5¼"
16 count	5½" x 4½"
18 count	5" x 4"

DAISIES

RIT® DYE POWDER COLORS NEEDED

◊ Lemon Yellow

◊ Kelly Green

◊ Dark Green

◊ Evening Blue Liquid Dye

◊ Royal Blue

PREPPING YOUR FABRIC

Cut a piece of 14 count White Aida 12½"w x 12½"h. Stitch count is 87w x 89h; work basting stitches to define dye area. Wash, rinse and press.

MIXING THE DYE

COLOR	DYE	WATER	SALT
lemon yellow & kelly green	1 teaspoon & ⅛ teaspoon	1 cup	1 teaspoon
kelly green	1 teaspoon	1 cup	1 teaspoon
dark green	1 teaspoon	1 cup	1 teaspoon
evening blue	4 teaspoons	1 cup	1 teaspoon
royal blue	1 teaspoon	1 cup	1 teaspoon

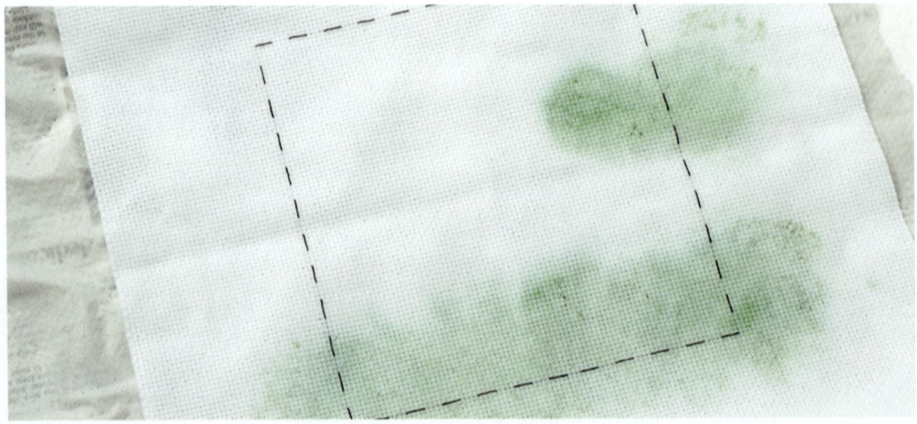

ONE Beginning with lemon yellow/kelly green, dab dye on the lower portion of the fabric. Dab lemon yellow/kelly green along the center right edge.

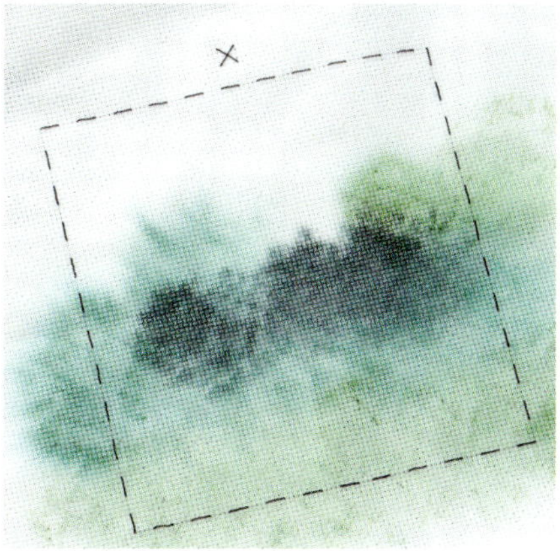

TWO Dab kelly green between the lemon yellow/kelly green sections on the right hand side then across the center of the fabric. Dab some dark green to the areas on each side between the lemon yellow/kelly green and kelly green.

THREE Dab evening blue across the top portion of the fabric and down left side to meet the greens. Dab royal blue across the center top portion of the fabric and down to meet the greens.

FOUR Allow to dry overnight. You may add more dye if you wish, but be sure to dampen the fabric first and mix up new dye. When you are happy with the look of your fabric, set the dye. You are now ready to begin stitching.

Daisies

x	dmc	b'st	color
☆	blanc		white
V	151	/	rose
C	158		dk blue
4	164		lt green
7	165		yellow green
◆	208		purple
#	327	/	dk purple
♥	600		vy dk pink
Z	602		dk pink
X	603		pink
O	604		lt pink
*	720		dk orange
$	741		orange
+	743		dk yellow
=	745		yellow
1	772		vy lt green
▲	986	/	dk green
8	988		green
/	3753		blue
	Grey area indicates last row of previous section of design.		

Design was stitched on a 12½" x 12½" piece of 14 count white Aida (design size 6¼" x 6½"). See Dyeing Instructions, pages 2-3. Three strands of floss were used for Cross Stitch and 1 strand for Backstitch.

stitch count (87w x 89h)

14 count	6¼" x 6½" "
16 count	5½" x 5¾"
18 count	5" x 5"

IRISES

RIT® DYE POWDER COLORS NEEDED

- ◊ Teal
- ◊ Golden Yellow
- ◊ Kelly Green
- ◊ Purple

PREPPING YOUR FABRIC

Cut a piece of 14 count White Aida 16"w x 13"h. Stitch count is 140w x 96h; work basting stitches to define dye area. Wash, rinse and press.

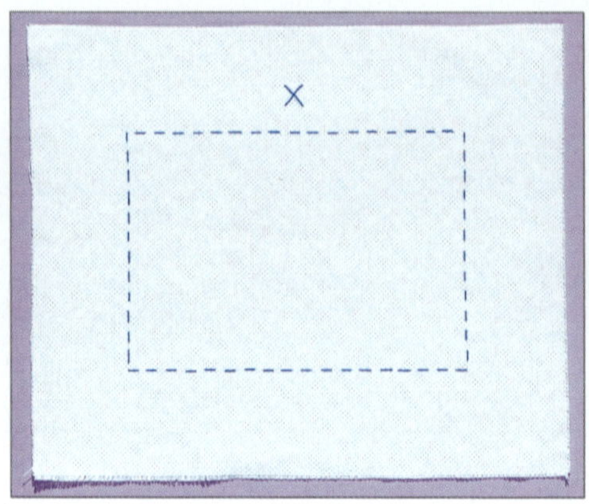

MIXING THE DYE

COLOR	DYE	WATER	SALT
teal	$^{1}/_{8}$ teaspoon	$1^{1}/_{4}$.cup	1 teaspoon
golden yellow & kelly green	1 teaspoon & $^{1}/_{2}$ teaspoon	1 cup	1 teaspoon
purple	$^{1}/_{8}$ teaspoon	1 cup	1 teaspoon

ONE Beginning with teal, dab dye on the left side and upper right corner of the fabric.

TWO Dab golden yellow/green mixture on right side of fabric, going down toward the center and back up to meet the teal. Dab golden yellow/green on bottom center of fabric.

THREE Add some purple to the area where the colors meet. Dab purple here and there. Make sure color extends at least 1" beyond basting threads.

FOUR Allow to dry overnight. You may add more dye if you wish, but be sure to dampen your fabric first and mix up new dye. When you are happy with the look of your fabric, set the dye. You are now ready to begin stitching.

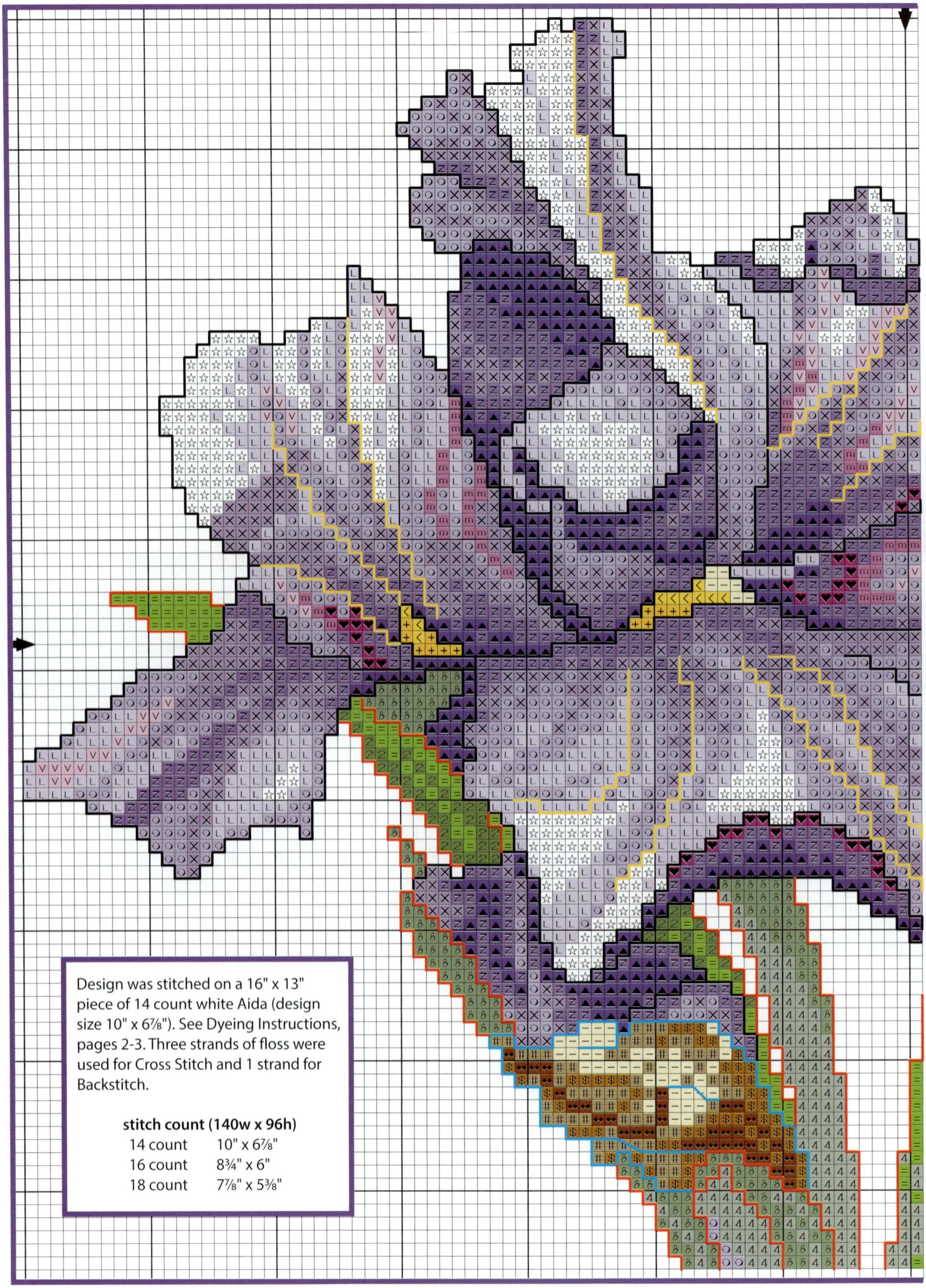

Design was stitched on a 16" x 13" piece of 14 count white Aida (design size 10" x 6⅞"). See Dyeing Instructions, pages 2-3. Three strands of floss were used for Cross Stitch and 1 strand for Backstitch.

stitch count (140w x 96h)

14 count	10" x 6⅞"
16 count	8¾" x 6"
18 count	7⅞" x 5⅜"

Irises

x	dmc	b'st	color
☆	blanc		white
L	211		vy lt purple
=	470		yellow green
8	520	/	dk green
4	522		grey green
▲	550	/	vy dk purple
Z	552	/	dk purple
X	553		purple
O	554		lt purple
+	742		dk yellow
<	743		yellow
−	745		lt yellow
2	937		green
♥	3607		dk fuchsia
m	3608		fuchsia
V	3609		lt fuchsia
$	3776		orange
#	3827		lt orange
◆◆	3858	/	rosewood

Grey area indicates last row of previous section of design.

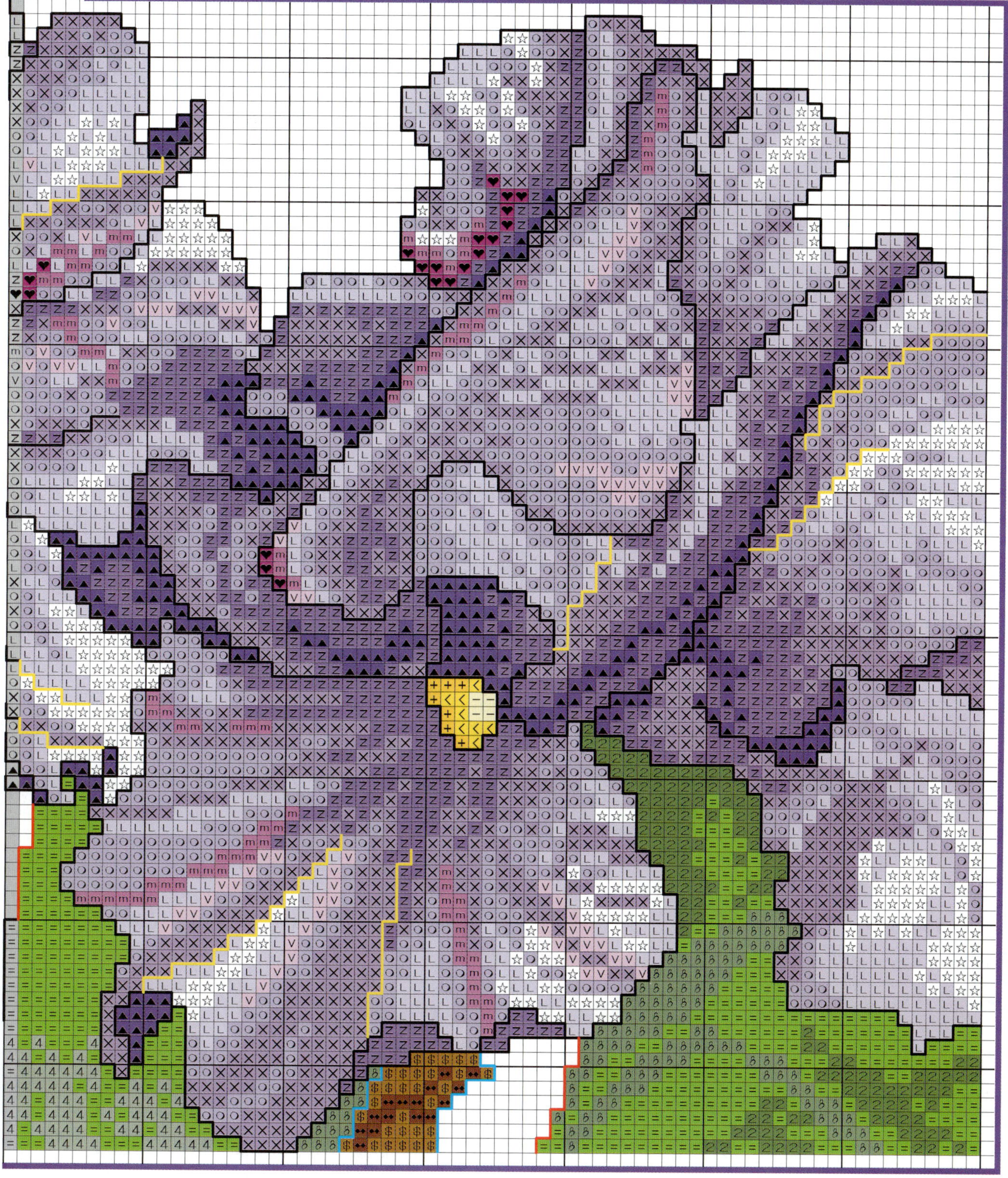

SUNFLOWERS

RIT® DYE POWDER COLORS NEEDED

- ◊ Purple
- ◊ Royal Blue

PREPPING YOUR FABRIC

Cut a piece of 14 count White Aida 12$^1/_2$"w x 15"h. Stitch count is 91w x 125h; work basting stitches to define dye area. Wash, rinse and press.

MIXING THE DYE

COLOR	DYE	WATER	SALT
purple (lavender)	1 teaspoon	1 cup	1 teaspoon
purple	1 teaspoon	$^1/_2$ cup	1 teaspoon
royal blue	1 teaspoon	1 cup	1 teaspoon

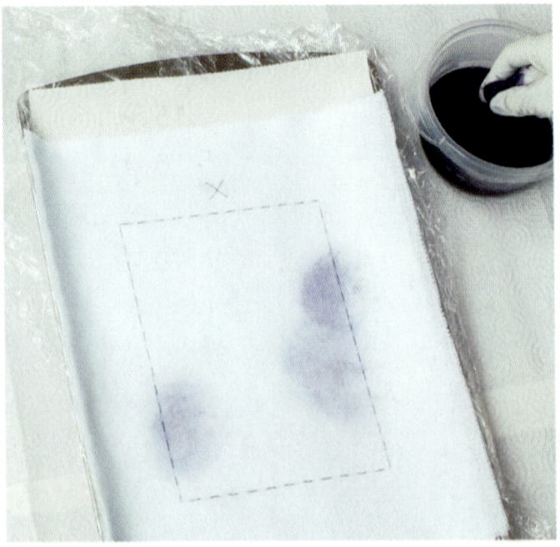

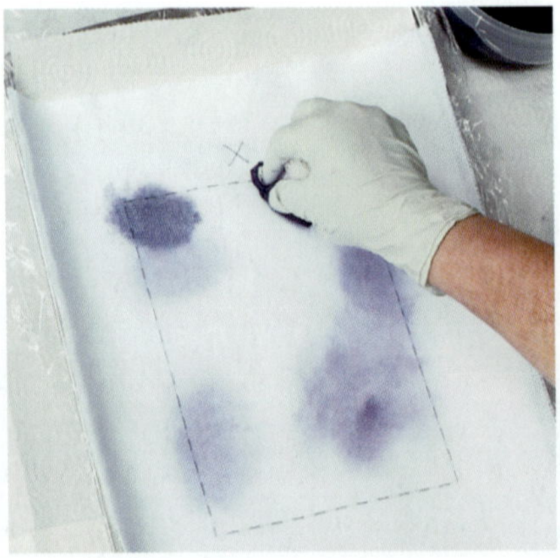

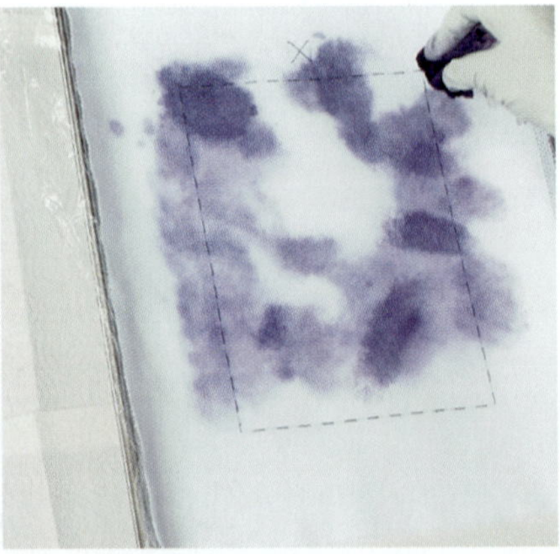

ONE Beginning with lavender, dab dye on the right side of the fabric. Dab lavender dye down toward center along the right edge. Add some lavender to the lower left corner.

TWO Dab purple in upper left corner of fabric, upper right corner, along right edge, and between lavender areas. Gently rub to blend colors.

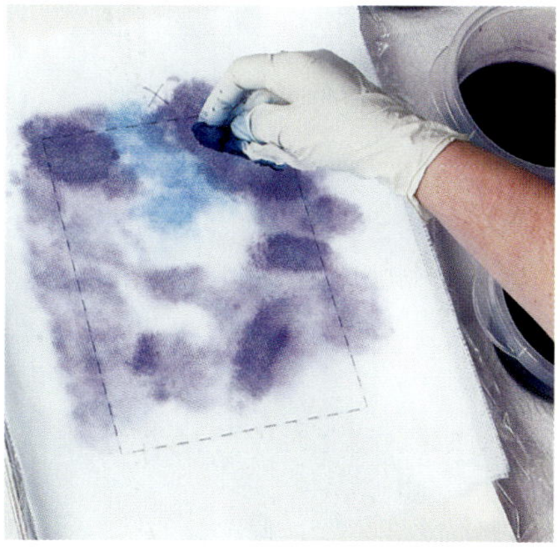

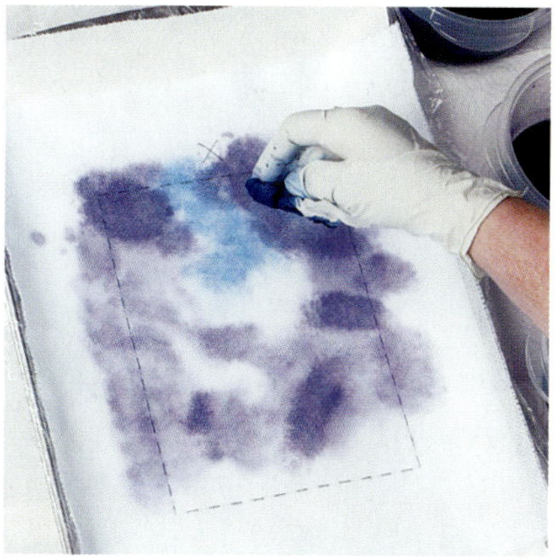

THREE Add some royal blue to the areas where the colors meet. Dab royal blue here and there along outer edges and center of design area. Make sure color extends at least 1" beyond basting threads.

FOUR Allow to dry overnight. You may add more dye if you wish, but be sure to dampen your fabric first and mix up new dye. When you are happy with the look of your fabric, set the dye. You are now ready to begin stitching.

Design was stitched on a 12½" x 15" piece of 14 count white Aida (design size 6½" x 9"). See Dyeing Instructions, pages 2-3. Three strands of floss were used for Cross Stitch and 1 strand for Backstitch.

stitch count (91w x 125h)

14 count	6½" x 9"
16 count	5¾" x 7⅞"
18 count	5⅛" x 7"

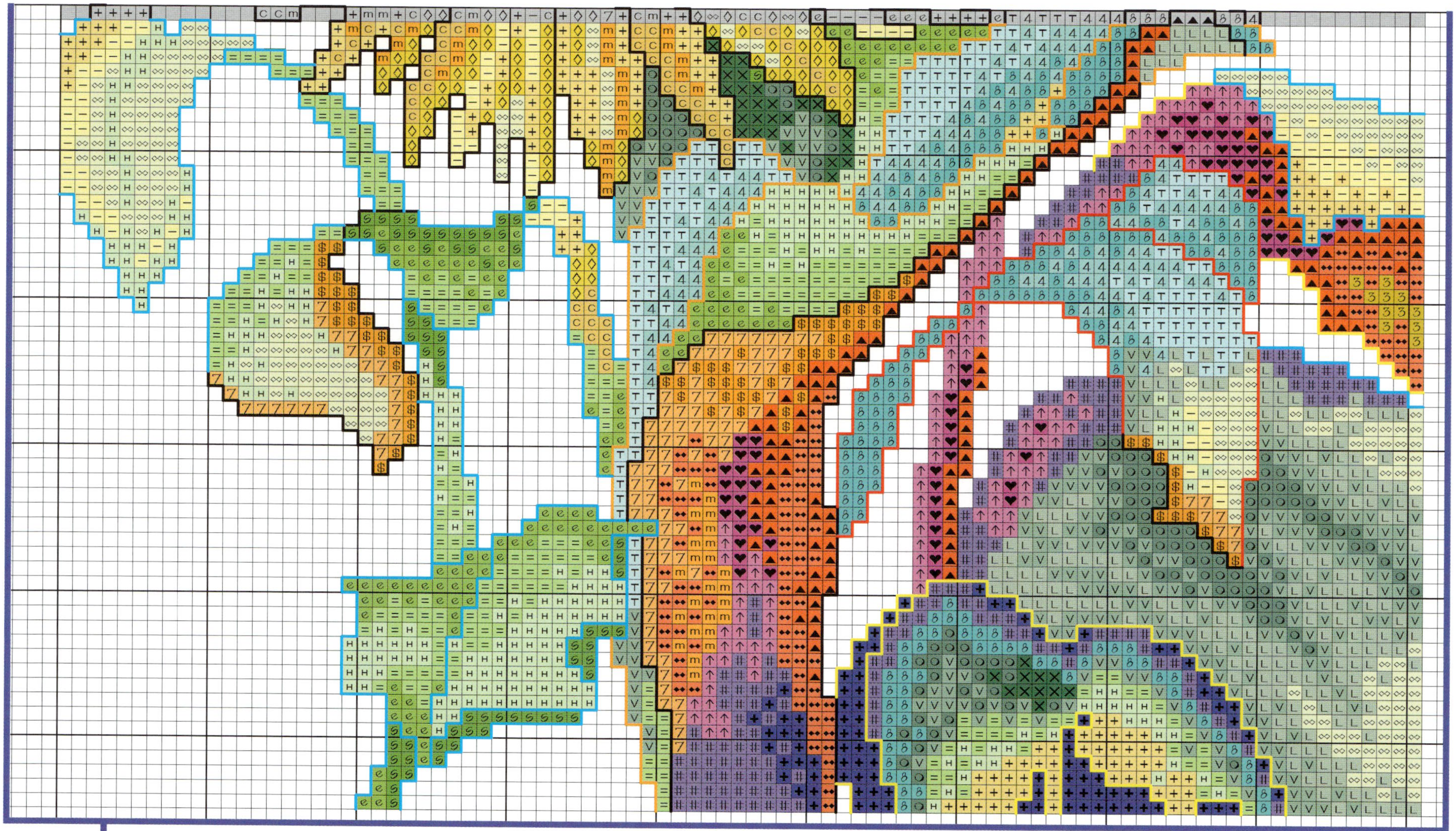

Sunflowers

x	dmc	b'st	color
O	320		blue green
X	367	/ (orange)	dk blue green
V	368		lt blue green
L	369		vy lt blue green
S	469	/ (blue)	dk yellow green
e	470	/ (purple)	yellow green
=	471		lt yellow green
H	472		vy lt yellow green
$	720		dk orange
7	721		orange
◇	725		dk yellow
+	726		yellow
−	727		lt yellow
C	728		vy dk yellow
3	783		gold
✚	791	/ (yellow)	navy
▲	920	/ (black)	dk orange
◆	922		orange
8	926	/ (red)	dk grey blue
4	927		grey blue
T	928		lt grey blue
∞	3078		vy lt yellow
♥	3687		rose
#	3746		purple
↑	3835		dk mauve
m	3854		lt orange

Grey area indicates last row of previous section of design.

TULIPS

RIT® DYE POWDER COLORS NEEDED

◊ Teal

◊ Royal Blue

◊ Purple

PREPPING YOUR FABRIC

Cut a piece of 14 count White Aida 11"w x 15$^{1}/_{2}$"h. Stitch count is 66w x 127h; work basting stitches to define dye area. Wash, rinse and press.

MIXING THE DYE

COLOR	DYE	WATER	SALT
teal	$^{1}/_{8}$ teaspoon	1$^{1}/_{4}$ cups	1 teaspoon
royal blue	$^{1}/_{4}$ teaspoon	1 cup	1 teaspoon
purple	1 teaspoon	$^{1}/_{2}$ cup	1 teaspoon

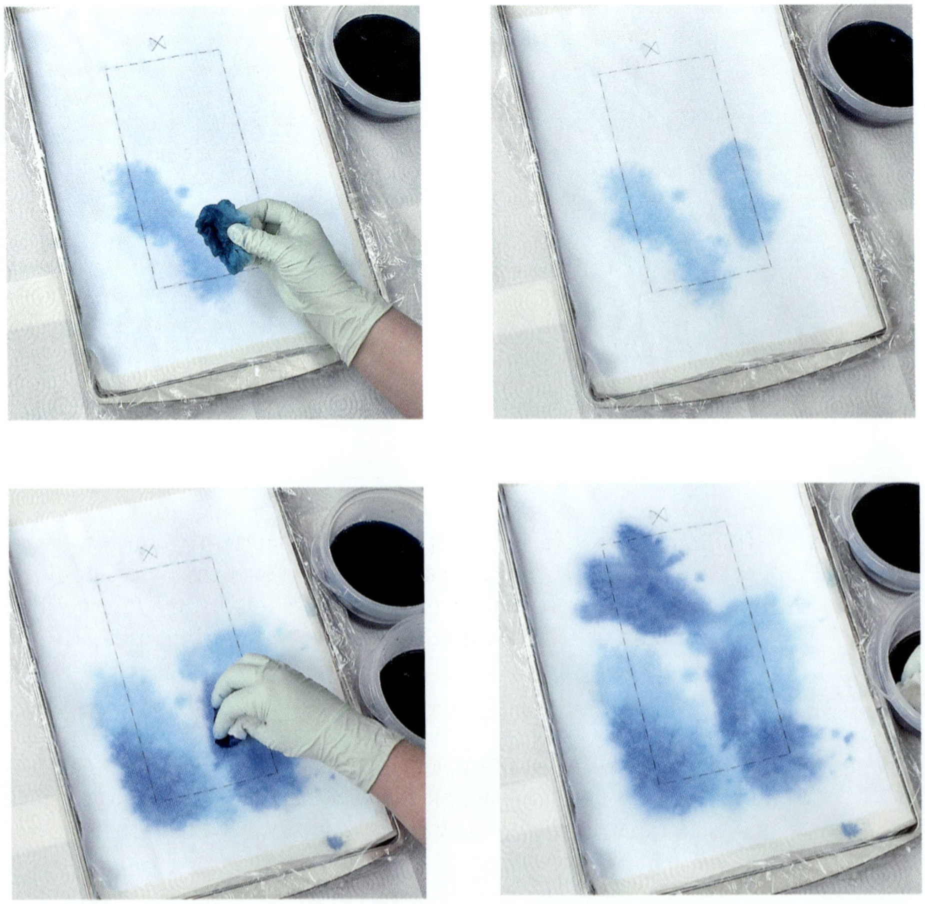

ONE Beginning with teal, dab dye on the lower half of the fabric sides and then toward the center.

TWO Dab royal blue at the bottom corners of the fabric and between teal areas. Add royal blue to the upper left corner and the upper center.

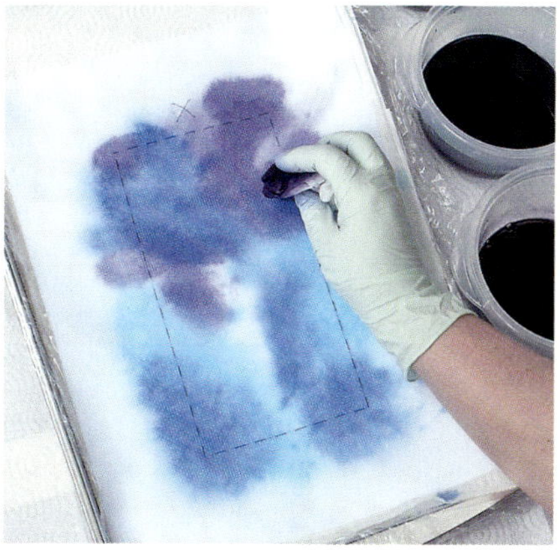

THREE Dab purple on the top third of the fabric. You may wish to blend the royal blue and purple together just a bit. Add just a hint of purple to white areas at the top of the fabric. Make sure color extends at least 1" beyond basting threads.

FOUR Allow to dry overnight. You may add more dye if you wish, but be sure to dampen your fabric first and mix up new dye. When you are happy with the look of your fabric, set the dye. You are now ready to begin stitching.

Tulips

x	dmc	b'st	color
◆◆	349	⁄ (blue)	vy dk coral
Z	350		dk coral
X	351		coral
O	352		lt coral
V	353		vy lt coral
+	472		yellow green
▲	700	⁄	green
$	702		lt green
⁒	704		vy lt green
★	712		cream
S	743		dk yellow
m	744		yellow
a	745		lt yellow
=	911		dk emerald
✳	912		emerald
L	948		peach
◇	959		blue green
⁄	964		lt blue green
#	967		vy lt orange
8	3340		orange
4	3341		lt orange
(grey)	Grey area indicates last row of previous section of design.		

Design was stitched on an 11" x 15½" piece of 14 count white Aida (design size 4¾" x 9⅛"). See Dyeing Instructions, pages 2-3. Three strands of floss were used for Cross Stitch and 1 strand for Backstitch.

stitch count (66w x 127h)

14 count	4¾" x 9⅛"
16 count	4⅛" x 8"
18 count	3¾" x 7⅛"

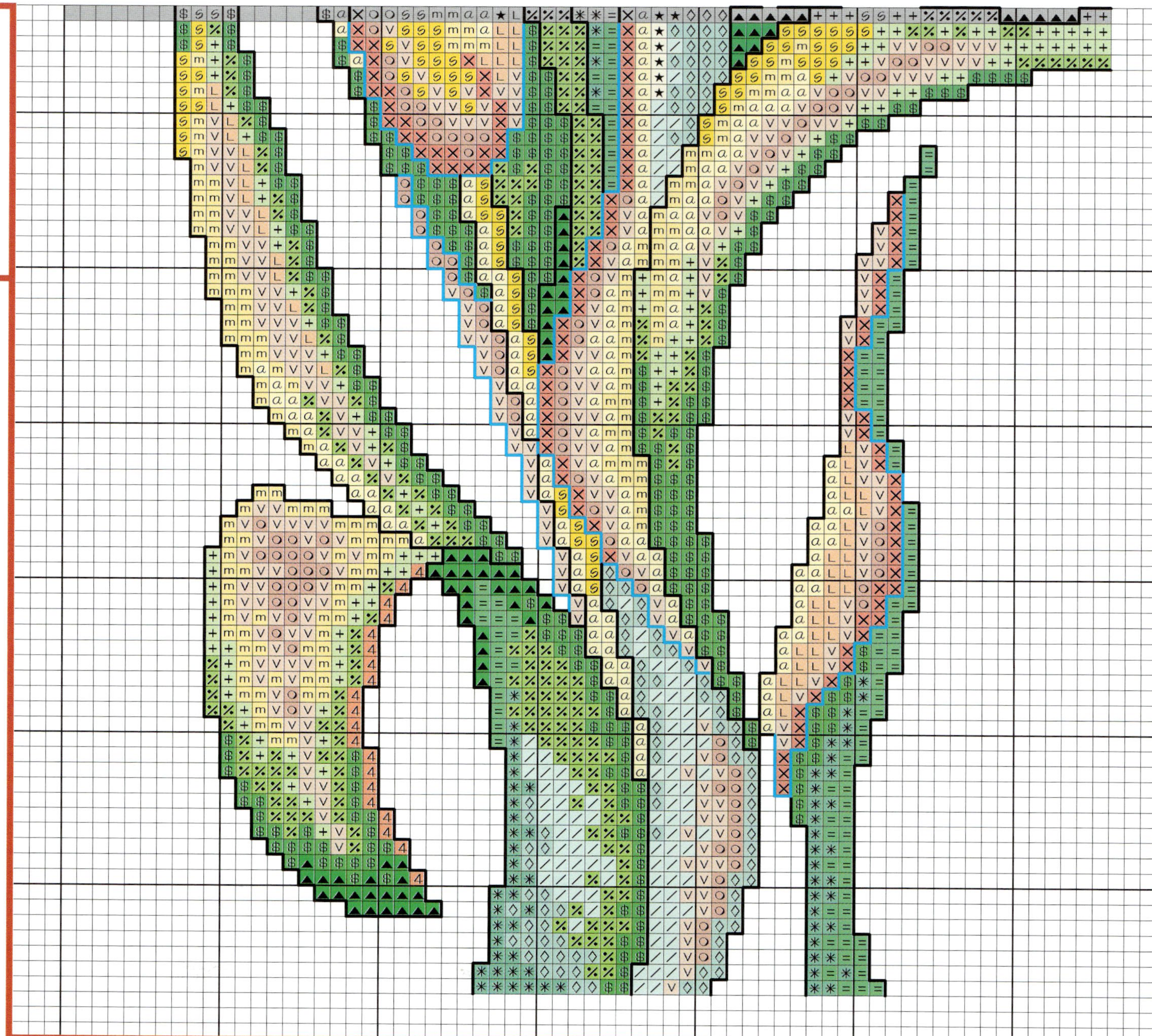

POPPIES

RIT® DYE POWDER COLORS NEEDED

◊ Evening Blue Liquid Dye

◊ Teal

◊ Kelly Green

◊ Dark Green

PREPPING YOUR FABRIC

Cut a piece of 14 count White Aida 14"w x 12"h. Stitch count is 108w x 83h; work basting stitches to define dye area. Wash, rinse and press.

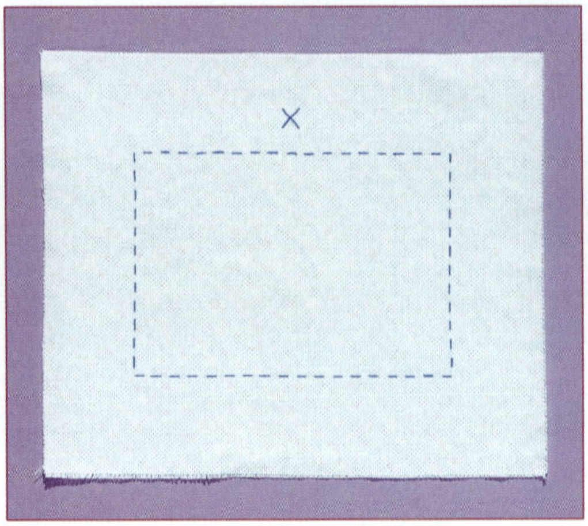

MIXING THE DYE

COLOR	DYE	WATER	SALT
teal	1 teaspoon	1 cup	1 teaspoon
dark green	1 teaspoon	1 cup	1 teaspoon
evening blue & kelly green	4 teaspoons & 1/2 teaspoon	1 cup	1 teaspoon

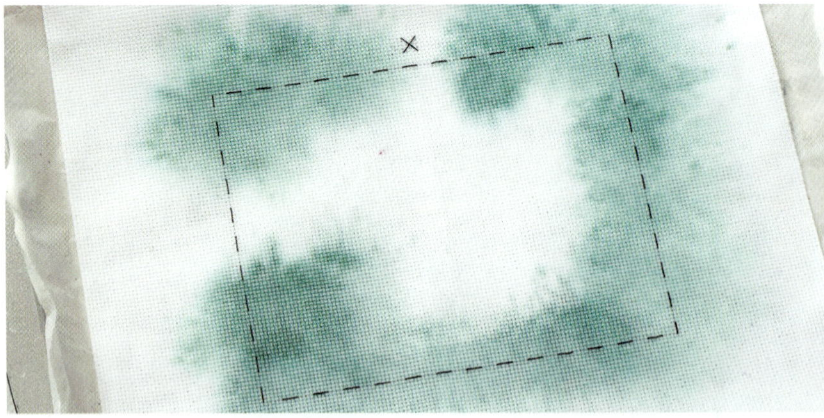

ONE Beginning with teal, dab dye across the bottom edge of the fabric, up the right side then across the top to slightly before the center. Dab dye from the lower left side of the fabric to slightly before the center and from the top left to slightly before the center.

TWO Dab dark green between teal areas.

THREE Dab evening blue/kelly green at the center top and center left side of the fabric. Make sure color extends at least 1" beyond basting threads.

FOUR Allow to dry overnight. You may add more dye if you wish, but be sure to dampen the fabric first and mix up new dye. When you are happy with the look of your fabric, set the dye. You are now ready to begin stitching.

Poppies

x	dmc	b'st	color
1	165		lt yellow green
=	166		yellow green
♣	349		lt red
Z	350		dk salmon
X	351		salmon
O	352		lt salmon
$	580		avocado green
#	581		dk yellow green
L	741		bright orange
a	743		yellow
♥	817		red
8	904		dk green
4	905		green
7	906		lime green
/	972		dk yellow
+	3340		orange
C	3768	/	blue grey
V	3825		lt orange
(grey)	Grey area indicates last row of previous section of design.		

Design was stitched on a 14" x 12" piece of 14 count white Aida (design size 7¾" x 6"). See Dyeing Instructions, pages 2-3. Three strands of floss were used for Cross Stitch and 1 strand for Backstitch.

stitch count (108w x 83h)

14 count	7¾" x 6"
16 count	6¾" x 5¼"
18 count	6" x 4¾"

GENERAL INSTRUCTIONS

HOW TO READ CHARTS

Each chart is made up of a key and a gridded design in which each square represents a stitch. The symbols in the key tell which floss color to use for each stitch in the chart. The following headings and symbols are given:

X – Cross Stitch
DMC – DMC color number
B'ST – Backstitch
COLOR – the name given to the floss color in that chart

A square filled with a color and a symbol should be worked as a Cross Stitch.

A straight line should be worked as a Backstitch.

A large dot listed near the end of the key should be worked as a French Knot.

Sometimes the symbol for a Cross Stitch may be partially covered when a Backstitch crosses the square. Refer to the background color to determine the floss color.

Though not listed separately in the key, a triangle filled with color and a reduced symbol (◪) in the chart is usually worked as a Quarter Stitch.

Always work Cross Stitches and Quarter Stitches first and then add the Backstitch and French Knots. When stitching, bring threaded needle up at 1 and all odd numbers and down at 2 and all even numbers.

Cross Stitch (X): For horizontal rows, work stitches in two journeys **(Fig. 1)**. For vertical rows, complete each stitch as shown **(Fig. 2)**.

Fig. 1

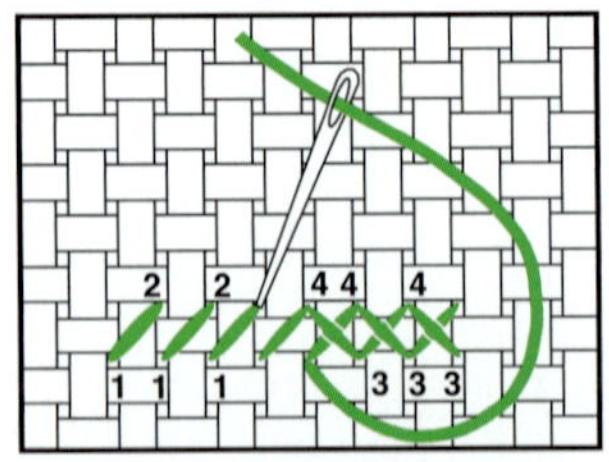

Fig. 2

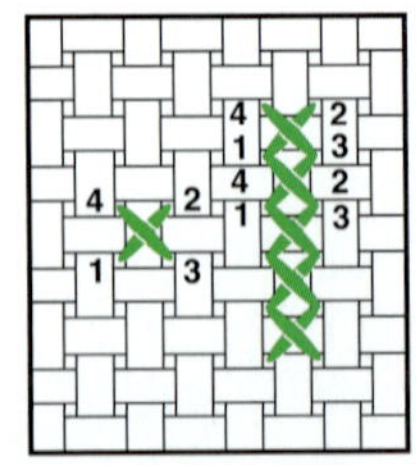

Quarter Stitch ($^1/_4$X): Come up at 1, then split fabric thread to go down at 2 **(Fig. 3)**.

Fig. 3

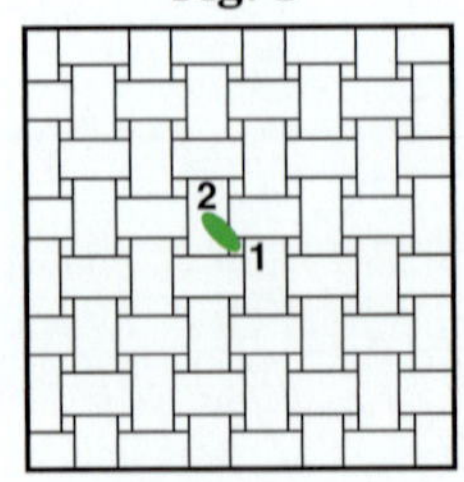

Backstitch (B'ST): For outlines and details, Backstitch should be worked after the design has been completed **(Fig. 4)**.

Fig. 4

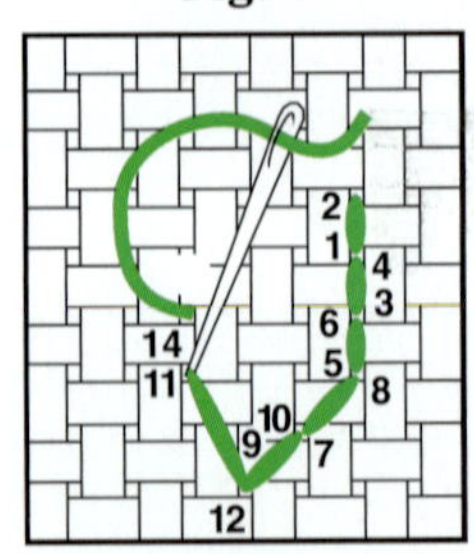

French Knot: Bring needle up at 1. Wrap floss once around needle. Insert needle at 2, tighten knot, and pull needle through fabric, holding floss until it must be released **(Fig. 5)**. For a larger knot, use more floss strands; wrap only once.

Fig. 5

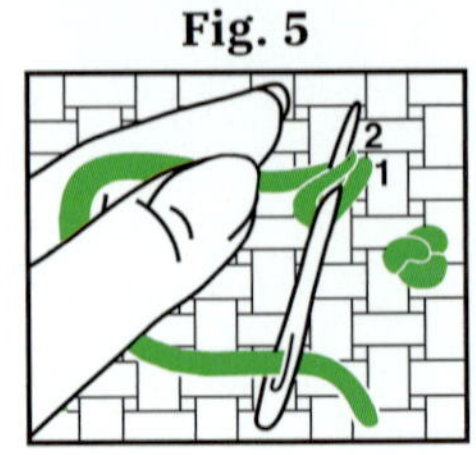

Photography setting images (Drifter Studio Print Shop) used under license from Creative Market.

Library of Congress Control Number: 2019933136

Copyright © 2019 by Leisure Arts, Inc., 104 Champs Blvd., STE 100, Maumelle, AR 72113, www.leisurearts.com. All rights reserved. This publication is protected under federal copyright laws. Reproduction or distribution of this publication or any other Leisure Arts publication, including publications which are out of print, is prohibited unless specifically authorized. This includes, but is not limited to, any form of reproduction on or through the Internet, including posting, scanning, or e-mail transmission.

We have made every effort to ensure that these instructions are accurate and complete. We cannot, however, be responsible for human error, typographical mistakes, or variations in individual work.

Made in U.S.A.